What people are saying about Your Passport to Freedom

"The topics covered in this book are vital for every Christian to know about, and to deal with. Too many people have remained ignorant of the effects of curses and the demonic in their lives, and those of their families.

Sharon Parkes is one of a growing number of Christian leaders awake to these issues, and is bringing effective Bible-based teaching to the attention of the Christian community.

My prayer is that this book will be used fruitfully to set many free across the world.

I have known Sharon and her husband Bob for some years, and we have ministered together, and I commend them to the reader."

> **Dr. Selwyn Stevens Ph.D.; D.Min;**
> **President: Jubilee Resources Intl. Inc.**
> **Wellington, New Zealand**

"As the movement toward powerful and widespread deliverance ministry continues to mushroom God keeps providing more and more tools for the task. One of the newest and most dynamic is *Passport to Freedom*. I love this book because Sharon Parkes gives us such practical advice for getting the job done!"

> **Doris Wagner, Founding Apostle**
> **International Society of Deliverance Ministers**

"Over the last ten years, Sharon Parkes has been employing the principles in this book to see many people set free by the power of the principles of God's Word. She and her husband, Bob, have raised up teams of people, both in our church as well as many churches around the world, who are equipped to bring many into the freedom purchased for us by the sacrifice of Christ on the cross. These principles work! As you read, allow God to activate His prophetic power in your life so that not only will you come to a new experience of liberty, but will also sense the call to set others free as well. 'Whom the Son sets free is free indeed!'"

> **Dr. Jane Hamon**
> **Co-Pastor Christian International Church**
> **Author, *The Debra Company*, *The Cyrus Decree* *and Dreams and Visions***

"The ministry of deliverance is key to living a victorious Christian life today. In *Passport to Freedom*, Sharon Parkes equips us to use the biblical pattern of deliverance ministered by Jesus himself. Let us follow Him into freedom!"

> **Dr. Sheryl L. Price**
> **Aligned for His Glory Network**
> **New Gretna, New Jersey**

Your Passport to Freedom

Deliverance Made Simple

By Sharon Parkes

Your Passport to Freedom
Deliverance Made Simple

Copyright © 2010 by Sharon Parkes
Printed in the United States of America

No part of this publication may be reproduced, stored in a retrieval system, or transmitted in any form by any means – electronic, mechanical, digital photocopy, recording, or any other without the prior permission of the author.

All rights reserved solely by the author. The author guarantees all contents are original and do not infringe upon the legal rights of any other person or work. No part of this book may be reproduced in any form without the permission of the author. The views expressed in this book are not necessarily those of the publisher.

All Scripture quotations are taken from the New King James Version of the Holy Bible unless indicated otherwise.

Table of Contents

Dedication	ii
Foreword	iii
Introduction	vii

Chapter 1
   Deliverance is Not Counseling   1

Chapter 2
   What are demons and how do they affect us?   15

Chapter 3
   How do we minister deliverance?   23

Chapter 4
   Forgiveness: A Key to Deliverance   35

Chapter 5
   Understanding Generational Curses   41

Chapter 6
   What is Freemasonry?   47

Chapter 7
   Deliverance Brings Healing   73

Chapter 8
   The Healing Centre – Beulah Restoration Centre   93

Chapter 9.
   My Testimony of Restoration   103

Chapter 10
   The Prayers   109

Dedication

First to the Lord for loving me so much and restoring to me everything the devil stole plus so much more.

I want to dedicate this book to my husband Bob who labors with me in this awesome ministry when you could be out fishing. You always encourage me to be all that God has called me to be. Also for reminding me that it was important to write the book to bring truth to the body of Christ.

To my sons; Del, Daniel and Kevin, my daughter-in-law Cayce and my grandchildren Ashton and Clara, you are my joy. Thank you for being so unselfish as to share me with the world.

I want to thank Lauranna Pridham for helping with the editing process. I am also grateful to you and Lynn Wambolt for taking the time to pray for the book and our ministry. You are fellow comrades in the War against the enemy.

Foreword

The discussion on deliverance for Christians brings up many questions in Christendom. If you have questions about deliverance from demonic activity or a desire to help people receive deliverance, then you have come to the right place. This book will help you understand the teaching and ministry of Jesus in bringing deliverance to God's people.

Sharon Parkes does not present a lot of philosophy and book learning about deliverance. She has done a lot of research both in the Bible and in writings of the best in this field. However, her greatest ability has come from experience in passionately giving herself to ministering deliverance to thousands of God's people. She has personally experienced real deliverance which has brought major victories and transformation to her life. She has great compassion for people who have problems caused by demonic activity, but she has no mercy for the demons. She has a powerful anointing and revelation that enable her to set people free and see their lives transformed by the power of God. She can transport people to freedom.

In my fifty-six years of ministry I have seen all the different ways people have sought to minister deliverance to God's people. Some have been biblically balanced and very effective. However, I have seen some saints and ministers who were very weird and what I call spooky-spiritual in the way they sought to minister deliverance. Let me assure the reader that the need for deliverance from demonic activity is biblically revealed and experientially real. My first years of Christianity were in a Pentecostal denomination that taught their people that Christians could not have demonic activity in their lives. They based this on their teaching that demons cannot cross the blood line. Therefore, if a person had once been cleansed by the blood of Jesus then they had permanent protection against any demon having access to them.

However, my first exposure and experience in casting out demons came as a surprise to me. When I came out of Bible College, a fellow student and I started evangelizing together. We held a seven-week revival in a local church where I stayed on as pastor. One night after my co-evangelist had preached and prayed for the people he became very despondent. A very powerful spiritual lady tried to encourage him. She finally asked me to come and help her pray for him. I casually came over and laid hands on his head and started praying for him. The anointed Sister started praying powerfully in the spirit. Suddenly, he started speaking in a guttural sound saying "I am going to kill you." I opened my eyes and saw that he was stretching forth his hands to strangle me. His eyes rolled back in his head and I started praying seriously. During the next three hours we cast five demons out of him. They told us their names and when and how they had come into him, after we had commanded them to do so.

Later in our discussion he admitted that he was a practicing homosexual for four years before he came to Bible College. He said he was inactive while in Bible College, and he had never manifested any of that toward me. He had been born again and his sins washed away by the blood of Jesus before coming to Bible College, but no one had ministered deliverance to him to set him free from that demonic influence and stronghold in his life. That experience adjusted my thinking concerning whether Christians could have demonic activity in their lives. People have asked me, "Can Christians have demons?" I usually say, "I have discovered that Christians can have about anything they want." If a Christian continually commits acts of the lust of the flesh, the lust of the eyes or the pride of life, they open the door and give Satan a legal right to send a demon to inhabit that area of their life to keep them in bondage. When this happens to a Christian, they normally need the ministry of deliverance to get set free.

Sharon takes the confusion and mystery out of the ministry of deliverance. She makes it simple and real. She simply shows the authority believers have to cast out demons and the sound and simple way it can be done. It is not something Christians should seek to do without good biblical teaching and some training. That is one reason why Sharon and her husband Bob have written teaching manuals on deliverance and conduct seminars on biblical deliverance.

I have known Sharon and Bob for many years. They are ordained ministers in the Christian International Apostolic Network which makes me their Bishop. They live on Hamon Avenue with us and many other church staff members. Their life and ministry are highly commendable. The truths and life experiences found within this book will bring revelation and transformation to the reader enabling them to be delivered and to minister deliverance to others. This book is a must read for everyone who wants to walk in deliverance and also minister deliverance to others.

Sharon, God's blessings are upon you, your family and your ministry for taking the time to write this book and share the great anointing, revelation, and ministry of deliverance that God has developed in your life. You are truly an extension of the anointing Jesus had to open the prison doors and set the captives free.

>Your Bishop: Dr. Bill Hamon
>Founder of C I Apostolic Network (CIAN)
>Author of ten major books including,
>*The Day Of The Saints*

Introduction

I have received several prophetic words about writing a book. I thought the book was to be on our experiences in teaching and ministering in the area of Deliverance. Rhidian Brooks, a friend from England said to me, "I see several books in you," so I had wanted to do the book but did not know where to begin, and was it to be my testimony or experiences in deliverance? In a friend's living room in England the Lord spoke to me again about writing the book on deliverance. At the time I was reading a flyer on a deliverance conference being held in London, England. I read the information about the conference and the different workshops, and what I felt was that this was not deliverance but psychology counseling. That is when the Lord spoke to me about writing a book about doing deliverance just the way he did it. He gave me the name *Deliverance Made Simple*. I shared this with my husband, Bob, and he immediately saw the picture of a passport and said he thought it was to be called *Passport to Freedom/Deliverance Made Simple*. I have already written two training manuals. One is called *Prophetic Deliverance and Restoration*, which has been translated into Spanish and German. And the other is called *Deliverance in the Marketplace,* and we use them to train healing and deliverance teams. But now it is time to write the book on healing and deliverance. I hope this book not only brings revelation about deliverance, and how it is an important and vital ministry necessary for the church today, but also that it will point out that we have a pattern in the

New Testament of how we should be doing and ministering deliverance. I believe that knowledge brings revelation.

Chapter 1
Deliverance is Not Counseling

What I have seen as we have traveled to many different countries and in the United States is that many churches have what they call a deliverance ministry. Once again what I found out is that it is really counseling. In this ministry of counseling they have brought in psychology and have called it deliverance. We have found that you cannot counsel out a demon, but you have to actually cast it out.

The purpose of this book is not to condemn other churches, deliverance ministers or ministries; it is to bring revelation that many of us are not doing deliverance. Yet what we are doing is bringing psychology counseling into the church and calling it deliverance.

I know this book may bring offense to many that are trying to do what they know to bring freedom to people. This is not our heart or intent. Just as Charles Finney stated when he received the knowledge about Freemasonry, that it was his duty and the duty of every Christian to expose the truth about it. We feel the same way about what is going on today with deliverance ministries. Some churches have brought in Deliverance ministry just because it is in mainstream churches, it sounds good, and it seems to work. They know they need help, but don't know who to turn to. Some have recognized that there is a need to set people free. Sometimes this revelation comes because of church members not being able to maintain their walk after prayer and counseling. Then the minister realizes that there is a demonic stronghold in the person's life that needs to be cast out. Many bring into the church what I call watered-down deliverance, one that pets the demons. Some have felt it is too controversial to bring in a true deliverance ministry. So they bring in a ministry that deals with the soulish area. But what I found is that they are adapting the world system of psychology and bringing it into the church. The Word of God says you shall know the truth and the truth will set you free. I believe when we show the difference between deliverance as Jesus did it, compared to man's emotional deliverance, that we will see many more set free and made whole. People will no longer have to struggle with issues in their lives that have been there for years and feel as though they can never be set free from them. We need to deal with the demons, not just emotions and thoughts. Many of these ministries teach that if you deal with the emotions and the thoughts, then people will be set free. What we have found is that when you cast out the demons it brings healing and wholeness to the emotions and thoughts. If you start by dealing with the emotions and the mind, this is where it ends up taking a long time to set the person free. Jesus did not do that. Why do we think we have to pattern deliverance after secular counseling and psychology? If we line up the way we minister to how Jesus did it we cannot go wrong. We need to get back to the simplicity of the Gospel.

We had a worship minister at our church on a Sunday whose name was Eddie James. Several of his team members gave testimonies of how they had been delivered. Some had been abused, raped and abandoned by their fathers, and they turned to drugs to escape the pain. One girl had begun cutting herself to escape the pain. But then God brought deliverance to them. Eddie said they didn't get free sitting in a room being motivated. He said that we don't need another self-help tip, what we need is to be delivered. He announced that God wanted to set people free. He then had his team of forty line up across the front of the church and they did a fire tunnel. For those of you who don't know what a fire tunnel is, some people call it a sheep dip. That is where two rows of people are formed, in this case there were forty, and then people begin to go through the line having hands laid on them as they proceed through the line. The Holy Spirit was moving and many were being touched. Could it be that simple? There is an old cliché that says; the proof is in the pudding. As people were going through the fire tunnel, some were weeping, some were laughing. Yes, people were being delivered as Eddie was on the platform and spoke to the demons and told them they had to go. And guess what, they obeyed him. It was incredible. They didn't have to wait and go through session after session of talking about what they were going through. I actually don't think it's very gracious to the person being ministered to having to wait week after week, sometimes month after month to be set free. All it does is stir up the demons that are in them and then they have to deal with the torment until the next appointment. Nowhere can I find in Scripture that it takes all that time, to be set free. Second Chronicles 29:36, *"then Hezekiah, and all the people rejoiced that God had prepared the people since the events took place so suddenly."* People will rejoice when we set them free quickly.

I want to share in this book about what the Lord has done in our ministry, in our lives, and the lives of others. Sharing the vision that the Lord gave us to do a quick work to get ready for the end time revival. When God releases revival that we've cried out for and thousands come into the church, we will not be able to spend a lot of time getting people set free. I want to have a sustained revival. Not a revival that starts and is aborted because people don't stay in the church after conversion. People come into the church and have a genuine conversion. But if they have not been delivered the demons pull them back out of church. For example, people come into the church and they have not been delivered of rejection. So they come to the altar and the Lord touches their heart, they say the sinner's prayer and receive Jesus in their heart, and they are now born again. Next Sunday they come to church and the rejection begins to speak to them. This is not such a friendly church. Nobody spoke to me today; they must think I'm not good enough. And maybe next Sunday, they decide not to come to church because they are not feeling accepted, so why go? Before you know it they are out of church again, no one is keeping them accountable and they backslide. Also like people who have addictions; they make a commitment, and give their heart to the Lord. They want to serve God, but they are still addicted to drugs or alcohol and they eventually fall away. The addictions control their lives so they are not able to be free. So why try to be a Christian? It is easier to give up. Sometimes they end up going deeper into drugs or alcohol because they feel hopeless and full of shame for not being able to give up the addictions.

The sustained revivals like the Argentine Revival show us what has been effective to keep the revival going. Carlos Anacondia, who is the evangelist in the Argentine Revival gets them saved, baptized in the Holy Spirit, and delivered at the same time. The same happens in Bogota, Colombia, China and Africa. Getting people delivered at the time of conversion is the key to seeing sustained revival. Now, we have seen people be instantly delivered when they accept the Lord, we've seen them delivered while under the anointing of worship and teaching. But for the most part, they actually have to have the demons cast out. In a Billy Graham crusade only 3 percent sustain their Christian walk. So we see there is a need to get people delivered at the time of conversion. I know I wished I had gotten delivered when I got saved. It would have made life a whole lot easier. The way these revivalists are doing deliverance is a quick work. They don't set up appointment after appointment. They are ministering to thousands. So, it is not possible with that many people to have a lot of deliverance sessions. Yet people are being set free by the thousands. It works. We see in the area of counseling and psychology that there are many sessions the person goes through in order to be free. That is not how Jesus did it, at times he spoke a word and people were set free. The comment to us when we say this has been done is that we are not Jesus. In the Word it says greater work, shall we do. John 14:12 says *"Most assuredly, I say to you he who believes in me the works that I do he will do also and greater works than these you would do because I go to my father."*

So I believe that we will get to the place of setting people free, with a word.

My husband Bob and I oversee the ministry of healing and deliverance for Dr. Bill Hamon's ministry, Christian International. We travel the nation training up churches and individuals in the area of healing and deliverance. We also have our own ministry, which is called Isaiah 62:4. The Lord gave us the ministry name of Isaiah 62:4, *"You shall no longer be termed forsaken, nor shall your land anymore be termed desolate. But you shall be called Hephzibah [God's delight], and your land Beulah [bride]; for the Lord delights in you. And your land shall be married."* Doesn't this sound like deliverance? People no longer feel forsaken or desolate, which means to feel abandoned, to give up, or to desert. Once they are set free they no longer feel this way. The Lord delights in them and they are His bride that He is coming back for without spot or blemish. He is not coming back for a bride that is beaten up and defeated or a bride that struggles with whom she is or that feels rejected and intimidated; full of fear instead of faith. No, He is coming back for the bride who knows she is an over comer and will be victorious, and that we have been given all authority and all power to speak to principalities and powers, and they must obey. If we have all power and authority then that leaves the devil with no power. The only power that the devil has is that which we hand over to him. I don't intend to hand anything over to him, especially any power or authority. When the Lord went to sit at the right hand of the Father, He gave that authority to us.

This authority is expressed as we train and do deliverance and we do not let the demons manifest. Luke 4:33-35 says,

"Now in the synagogue. There was a man who had a spirit of an unclean demon. And he cried out with a loud voice. [34]saying "let us alone! What have we to do with you, Jesus of Nazareth? Did you come to destroy us? I know who you are – the – Holy One of God. [35]But Jesus rebuked him saying, "Be quiet, and come out of him!" And when the demon had thrown him in their midst, it came out of him and did not hurt him." We do not let them put on a show. I tell people we do not do Hollywood deliverance. That is where people are foaming at the mouth, throwing up, being jerked around screaming, talking and manifesting. We simply tell them to be quiet. We always explain to the person being ministered to that we are not talking to them; we are speaking to the demon and telling it we won't put up with their manifestations. We tell the demon that the Spirit of God that lives within that person is stronger than them.

We have never seen manifestations do any good. If they are ripping and tearing it hurts the person and brings fear. It can also bring shame to the person being set free. We've seen ministers talk to demons, but we believe the demons have no truth in them. Just like their father the devil was the father of lies. We don't believe that you can make demons tell the truth, who they are and why they are there.

In the early years of our ministry the demons would manifest and try to act like they had some authority. When we launched our deliverance ministry at our local church there was a lady who had come to the service that night. After the teaching on deliverance, we called for the teams that we had trained to come forth and help us minister to the people. They were lined up in the aisles to be prayed for. So when this lady came up to us for prayer we laid hands on her to cast out a spirit of death because she was battling cancer and the demon threw her ten feet through the air. All the people waiting to be prayed for began to sit down out of fear. We ran over to the lady who landed in the aisle. She spoke in a manly voice. It said, "You cannot have her. She is mine." That is when the Lord spoke to us and said He had given us all authority and we didn't have to put up with the theatrics. We spoke to her spirit man, and we told her that the Spirit of God within her was stronger than this demon. We were able to cast a spirit of death out and set her free.

If we're going to see deliverance restored to the local church we need to see people trained and moving in their authority over the demons. Luke 10:19 says, *"behold I give you the authority to trample on serpents and scorpions and over all the power of the enemy and nothing shall by any means hurt you.* Matthew 10:1, *and when he had called his twelve disciples to him. He gave them power over unclean spirits, to cast them out and heal all kinds of sickness and all kinds of diseases."* When a person is free and delivered they are able to move in this kind of authority.

The intent of this book is to share what the Lord has done in our ministry, in our lives, and the lives of others. Sharing the vision that the Lord gave us to do a quick work to get ready for the end time revival. We see in the area of psychology that there are many sessions the person goes through in order to be free. But that is not how Jesus did it. At times He spoke a word and people were set free. Wow, can you imagine that? Speaking a word, and the demons all leave. The comment to us when we say this has been done is that we are not Jesus. But in the word it says greater work, shall we do. John 14:12 says, *"Most assuredly, I say to you he who believes in me the works that I do he will do also and greater works than these you would do because I go to my father"* (King James Version). So I believe that we will get to the place of setting people free, with a word. Actually I think it would be great if we walked into a room to minister to someone and the demons screamed and left. We could say "we're done here!" That would be a greater work.

There are many ministries that seem to be very popular and established in many churches. So I asked The Lord, "Why does it seem like there's such an open door for these ministries," and then the Lord said they are not a threat to the enemy. The way they minister to people is to question emotions and ask the people how they feel. What memory torments them? Our assistant that oversees the Healing and Deliverance teams here at the local church shared with me her experience in having this type of ministry. She said, "Many times, as we have been counseled by various wonderful Christian people, we've been prompted to go back and remember that (trauma, or painful memory of some sort). We were told to remember that feeling, the smells, and the sense of the moment of that time. After reading a word from Chuck Pierce, I believe that we were actually revisiting (not talking about simply remembering or looking back) the old times of wounding. We actually invite, maybe even enter into a type of conjuring up those demonic spirit realms that were involved initially, as well as stirring up the original emotion and reaction." Chuck Pierce was ministering at the Ignited Church in Lakeland, Florida. He was talking about entering a season of redeeming the time. He said that "God doesn't make us go back into our past. We can't go back in our past that is called spiritualism. You can't go back into your past and commune." Spiritualism is a monotheistic belief system or religion, postulating a belief in God, but with a distinguishing feature of belief that spirits of the dead residing in the spirit world can be contacted by mediums, which can then provide information about the afterlife.

Sometimes these ministers will have them visualize where the Lord is when these horrible things are happening. We experienced this firsthand years ago, when our son was having some struggles. A couple offered to minister to him and he agreed. We sat in on a session. They asked our son about any trauma in his life. He shared a horrible situation that happened to him as a teenager. They asked him to remember what had happened and begin to see it and go back to that situation. They asked him, "Can you see the situation?" He said yes. Then they told him to look for Jesus. They said Jesus was there when it happened. Our son said he could not see Jesus and also that there was no way Jesus could have been there and didn't help him. They continued to say to him, "Keep looking, he's there." After a while, our son said, "Oh yes he's there." Then, they told him to give the pain to Jesus, and he would take it to the cross. Our son told us afterwards that he just agreed with them so they would stop. We know many thousands of people go through this type of ministry. Some have said they have been set free by it, but we have also heard from many that were not set free. One minister said to me, "How can you say to someone that is being raped, that Jesus is right there watching it. It would be as if he has no power or desire to help that person." This is where we feel ministries have crossed over into some witchcraft and psychology/counseling and they are calling it deliverance.

What is psychology and where does it come from? The Webster's dictionary defines psychology as:

1. The science of the mind in any of its aspects.
2. The systematic investigation of human or animal behavior pattern of mental processes characteristic of an individual or type.

The word psychologizing means to theorize psychologically. It also means to interpret psychologically, to explain (behavior) in psychological terms.

They go into the area of the mind and deal with memories to get rid of the demons. As I have stated earlier they say this will help with the emotions once the mind is healed. But we have found when you cast the demons out, the mind and emotions are healed. You cannot set people free by using intellect, or a formula. The area of deliverance is done by the spirit, not by the mind. We are not able to set people free by reasoning in the mind, either our minds or theirs. The way Jesus set people free was to discern what was there and then cast it out. He never went into the emotional area. He moved in, the gifts of the word of knowledge, and discerning of spirits. He never asks them how they felt or did this bear witness with them. There is a part of our emotions that likes to communicate. We want to be heard, especially if we have ever been abused. This is not wrong. It is okay to share the things that we have been through. But letting someone tell all the things that they've been through, and then telling them to give it to the Lord is not deliverance. We have a pattern in the Scriptures set by Jesus himself on how to cast out devils and set people free. Jesus simply discerned what was there, called it by name and cast it out.

What is the gift of discernment? A precise definition is not possible with this gift. Hebrews 5:14 says, *"but solid food belongs to those who are full of age, that is, those who by reason of use have their senses exercised to discern both good and evil"* (KJV). What this is saying is that we have a supernatural ability to discern whether something is good or evil. We can determine what source it is coming from, whether it is from the Lord or is demonic. The word discerning in Greek is the word *Diakrisis*, which means to judge through. This implies in Greek, a piercing of all that is outward and seeing right through. I like that the definition of discernment in Greek means discerning of spirits is not based on what we see as much as what we sense in the spiritual realm. So when we are doing deliverance we do not have to ask the person what has been bothering them, tormenting them, or troubling them. We can discern what is there. Remember, discernment is a gift that we simply have to ask the Lord for; if we believe then we will receive it. Discerning of spirits comes through a flash of revelation in your thoughts, a mental impression through a prophetic flow. It is not human reasoning, but Holy Spirit, revelation. I also believe we have to step out in faith and use it to keep it active and sharp. We have found that many people don't even know why they behave the way they behave and do the things they do. They sometimes think they know, but that's where discernment comes in. Instead of asking them, the Holy Spirit just shows us what is there.

Another way we can know what demons are influencing the person is the gift of the Word of Knowledge. This is an operation of the gift of the Holy Spirit. You express and receive my faith. We have two examples in the Word of the

Word of Knowledge. In 1 Samuel 10:14-16 is where Saul's father's donkeys were lost, and Saul inquired of Samuel the Prophet to receive a word of knowledge about where the donkeys were.

Another example is in 1 Kings 14:1-6. *"At that time Abijah, the son of Jeroboam, became sick. ²And Jeroboam said to his wife please arise, and disguise yourself, that they may not recognize you asked the wife of Jeroboam, and go to Shiloh. Indeed Ahijah, the prophet is there, who told me that I would be King over this people. ³Also take with you 10 loaves, some cakes, and a jar of honey, and go to him. He will tell you what will become of the child. ⁴And Jeroboam's wife did so, she arose and went to Shiloh and came to the house of Ahijah. But Ahijah could not see, for his eyes were glazed by reason of his age. ⁵Now the Lord had said to Ahijah, "Here is the wife of Jeroboam coming to ask you something about her son, for he is sick. Thus and thus you shall say to her for it will be when she comes in, that she will pretend to be another woman. ⁶And so it was when Ahijah heard this sound of her footsteps as she came through the door, he said come in, wife of Jeroboam. Why do you pretend to be another person, for I have been sent to you with bad news."*

So the blind prophet had a word of knowledge that it was Jeroboam's wife, who was approaching the house. The word of knowledge can be helpful in deliverance to go right for root issues and the demons that are binding the person up. That is why we call our ministry *prophetic healing and deliverance*. It is just a different arm of the prophetic. Instead of saying a prophetic word for the person we discern what is there with the prophetic anointing and flowing with the gifts of the word of knowledge or discerning of spirits and set the person free. People are so amazed when they are ministered to, and God shows us when the enemy entered and took advantage of them. For example, we say that a spirit of rejection which entered when you were little, because there was favoritism in your family, we cast it out now. Another example, the Holy Spirit will show us that a spirit of betrayal entered into their first marriage because of adultery and we then cast it out. We don't always have to be this specific we could just call it out by what we are discerning is there and it has to go. We train our teams to not ask the person any questions. Once in a training class, a pastor from New York brought a list of the demons that the Lord had showed him he had. He gave me the list and told me he wanted to make sure everything on the list was dealt with. I told him to keep his list in his pocket. I told him I was sure the team would get everything that was on the list. To his amazement, they did. When Jesus died on the cross it was not just for our salvation, but for healing and deliverance also. So my faith is not in people, but it is in Jesus. I know he loves people enough that he will make sure they are set free. More than they want to be free and more than I want to see them set free. Jesus paid the price to do it. He will be faithful.

Chapter 2

What are demons and how do they affect us?

Webster's dictionary defines a demon as: an evil being: Devil or fiend, a persistently tormenting person, force.

Strong's concordance (1140) daimonion (dahee_mon_ee_on): a daemonic being, by extension, a deity (1142) daimon (dah'_ee-mown) from daio (to distribute fortunes); a daemon or supernatural spirit of a bad nature.

Vine's expository dictionary says this about demons: demons are the spiritual agents acting in all idolatry. The idol itself is nothing, but every idol has a "demon" associated with it, which induces idolatry, with its worship and sacrifices (1 Cor. 10:20-21; Rev. 9:20; Deut. 32:17; Isa. 13:21; 34; 14; 65:3, 11). They disseminate errors, among men, and seek to seduce believers (1 Tim. 4:1) the great apostasy. Now the Spirit expressly says that in latter times some will depart from the faith, giving heed to deceiving spirits and doctrines of demons. As seducing spirits they deceive men into the supposition that through mediums (those that have "familiar spirits" – see Lev. 20:6; Lev. 20:27) they can converse with deceased human beings. This is the destructive deception of spiritism, forbidden in Scripture (Lev. 20:6, 27). In Leviticus

19:31; Deuteronomy 18:11 and Isaiah 8:19; demons tremble before God (James 2:19). They recognize Christ as Lord, and as their future Judge (Matt. 8: 29; Luke 4:41). Christ cast them out of human beings by His own power. His disciples did so in His name and by exercising faith. (Matt. 17:20) Acting under Satan (Rev. 16:13) demons are permitted to inflict bodily disease. Luke 13:11-13; *"and behold there was a woman who had a spirit of infirmity for eighteen years and was bent over and could in no way raise herself up. ¹²But when Jesus saw her he called her to him and said to her, 'Woman you are loosed from your infirmity.' ¹³And He laid His hands on her and immediately she was made straight, and glorified God."* So demons cannot be in our spirit, but they can be in our body.

Being unclean they tempt human beings with unclean thought, (Matt. 10:1; Mark 5:2; 7:25; Luke 8:27-29; Rev. 16:13; 18:2) they differ in degrees of wickedness, (Matt.12:45) and they will instigate the rulers of the nations at the end of this age to make war against God (Rev. 16:1).

Many believers have a problem when we say that a Christian can have a demon. They think that a nonbeliever can have a demon, but if we have the Spirit of God in us how can a Christian also have a demon.

First Thessalonians 5:23; *"now may the God of peace himself sanctify you completely; and may your whole spirit, soul, and body be preserved blameless at the coming of our Lord Jesus Christ."*

Our spirit belongs to God; this is where the Holy Spirit resides. Demons cannot affect our spirit for our spirit belongs to the Lord. *"But if Christ is in you, your body is dead because of sin, yet your spirit is alive because of righteousness. And if the Spirit of him who raised Jesus from the dead is living in you"* (Rom. 8:10-11). Our spirit will live forever. But this Scripture in Thessalonians talks about our soul and our body. Our body is what we see when we look at a person; skin color, our hair or whether we are male or female. Our five senses are housed in our body: sight, sound, taste, touch, and smell. In our body we can be affected by demons. Can we have sickness in our body? Even though we have the Holy Spirit in us our body can be full of disease and racked with pain. We asked people, if you are sick is it in you or out of you? There is a demon called infirmity. Sickness and disease are not a fruit of the Spirit, and many Christians are struggling with infirmity in their bodies. We will cover this more in our chapter on healing.

The next area is the soul. The soul consists of our emotions, our mind, and our will. Emotions are a strong or intense feeling. Emotions include love, joy, fear, or anger. The demons can enter into our emotions and influence them. Have you ever met anyone whose emotions controlled them? For example, people who are dealing with depression. Depression affects the mind, but it also affects the emotions. *Then he said to them, "Go your way, eat the fat, drink the sweet, and send portions to those for whom nothing is prepared; for this day is holy to our Lord. Do not sorrow, for the joy of the LORD is your strength"* (Neh. 8:10). If depression is affecting their emotions, then they won't be able to experience joy.

We have our mind; the way we think or perceive things (the conscious and unconscious process of our brain) is called our reasoning capability. The last area in the soul is our will, which consists of our choices, and the subsequent actions of our decisions. For example, David was a willing (acting) and obedient (thinking) man. Our will is where we also have self-discipline and self-control. Our conscience is housed in our soul. Our conscience is what prompts us during moral conflicts of what is right and wrong. Sometimes the conscience gets seared because of hurts, and people are not able to differentiate what is right or wrong. We look at people who do horrible things. We ask how they could have done what they did. It's because the demons have affected their conscience.

We cannot be demon possessed. This is un-biblical because possession would mean that the demons own the person. But as we have just learned, a Christian can be tormented or oppressed in the body and soul-ish area. Ephesians 6:12 says Christians have to battle against principalities, against powers, against the rulers of the darkness of this world, and against spiritual wickedness in high places. These are demons. We are told in the Scriptures that we will come against these spirits. The good news is we have the authority to cast them out. What would you rather do; stay bound up because it doesn't fit your theology, or be set free? I have a little saying when I am talking to people about deliverance and being delivered, especially when they have a hard time thinking that a demon could be inside of them. I tell them that's not really why I am here. I'm not here to argue theology or make a point. I am just here to offer freedom to them. So I say to them "in or out, when in doubt cast it out" if they think the demon is sitting on their shoulder or head whispering in their ear. It doesn't matter. The question is do they want to be free? I heard a minister once say that he believes that there are demons that work in the area of theology to get us to argue and debate over this issue; rather than meeting the needs of the people. So this will keep the people bound up if they don't believe they have demons and we continue to try and fix them.

People ask where do demons come from? In Scripture it talks about demons but not specifically where they come from. There are a few schools of thoughts on this. One theory is that they are fallen angels. When Lucifer rebelled against God, there were angels that also rebelled and were cast out with him. Now these were either fallen angels or demons. *"For if God did not spare the angels who sinned but cast them down to hell and delivered them into chains of darkness to be reserved for judgment"* (2 Pet. 2:4). This Scripture implies that these fallen angels are in chains. Not walking around. They are in chains, waiting to be judged by the Lord. The other theory is the one from Genesis 6:4. *"There were giants in the earth in those days and also afterward, when the sons of God came into the daughters of men, and they bore children to them. Those were the mighty men who were old men of renown."* The theory is that these giants who are part human and part fallen angels are demons. The Bible does not say that these giants are demons. I personally believe they are just spiritual beings. I don't get too hung up on where they came from. You can ask several ministers where demons came from, and there would be many different answers. There are different answers because the Scriptures are not specific on their origin.

But we do know the demons or spirits do not have a body. That's why they want to be in our bodies. The word spirit comes from the word *Pneuma*. Pneuma primarily denotes the wind. To breathe, blow. A spirit is like the wind. It is invisible. Spirit-breath, Old Testament 7307 Ruach is a Hebrew word and it means breath, air, and spirit. Ruach Scripture reference for air is Job 41:16, Ruach Scripture reference for breath is Isaiah 42:5. Demons do not have a body, so they are spirits, like the wind, they may not be seen, but they are there.

We have, what we call the seventeen truths about demons.

1. They do exist.
2. They are spiritual beings without a body. So they need human bodies to operate in. Luke 24:39, *"Behold my hands and my feet, that it is I myself. Handle me and see, for a spirit does not have flesh and bones as you see I have."*
3. They ordinarily cannot be seen. But you can know they are there by the discerning of spirits.
4. They have super powers.
5. They have distinct personalities.
6. They are active throughout the world.
7. They are shown to have knowledge and can speak. Mark 1:24, *"Let us alone! What have we to do with you, Jesus of Nazareth, did you come to destroy us? I know who you are – the Holy One of God."*
8. They possess a will. Matthew 12:44, *"I will return to my house."*
9. They believe and have emotions. James 2:19, *"The demons also believe and tremble."*
10. They are organized under a strongman and Satan is that head.

11. They intend evil. They are not your friend.
12. They are unclean.
13. They don't want to be discovered, so they hide.
14. They can be in a Christian and in churches.
15. They cannot reproduce.
16. They are terrestrial beings. Webster's dictionary defines terrestrial as: of or relating to the earth. Living on our own land. Second Corinthians 5:1 *"upon earth, terrestrial, belonging to the earth, or on the earth,"* and as applied to bodies (1 Cor. 15:40); space to earthly things.[1] The biblical reference for terrestrial is Luke 11:24-26 and Matthew 12:43-45, *"when an unclean spirit goes out of a man, he goes through dry places, seeking rest, and finds none. ⁴⁴"Then he says, I will return to my house from which I came." And when he comes, he finds it empty, swept, and put in order. ⁴⁵Then he goes and takes with him seven other spirits more wicked than himself, and they enter and dwell there; and the last state of that man is worse than the first. So shall it also be that this wicked generation."* Walking through dry places refers to the earth. That is why after deliverance we have to fill the person back up with Godly things so there is no room for them to come back.
17. They are under Jesus' authority and must obey because they have been defeated by the blood of Jesus! This is the best part.

So now we have discussed what demons are and how they affect us. How can we be free of demons or set others free? The word deliverance is the act of delivering or state

---

[1] From Barnes' notes, electronic database copyright 1997, 2003, by Bible soft, Inc. All rights reserved.

of being delivered. We have received prophetic words that God has called us liberators. The word means to set us free from bondage, foreign occupation, to free from oppression. Part of the great commission for us as believers is not only getting people saved, but it is also to get them healed and delivered.

Mark 16:17-18, *"And these signs will follow those who believe: In My name they will cast out demons; they will speak with new tongues; [18]they will take up serpents; and if they drink anything deadly, it will by no means hurt them; they will lay hands on the sick, and they will recover."*

The Lord is coming back for his bride, one without spot or blemish. Are we that bride without spot or blemish? In order to move in the authority and freedom that Christ purchased for us we will need to be set free and free others. We do want to see our churches grow. We want to see the revival. Wolfgang Simpson, a German evangelist with signs following his ministry says that the three main ingredients to revival are healing, deliverance and the prophetic. Most churches do not have deliverance. We have people call from all over to ask if they can come to be delivered because there is not deliverance where they live or even in their church. We either direct them to other churches that we know of in their state or countries, or we have them come to Christian International to be ministered to. How this must grieve the Lord's heart. He paid a high price for the ministry of healing and deliverance and yet it is not so readily available to His children.

Chapter 3
How do we minister deliverance?

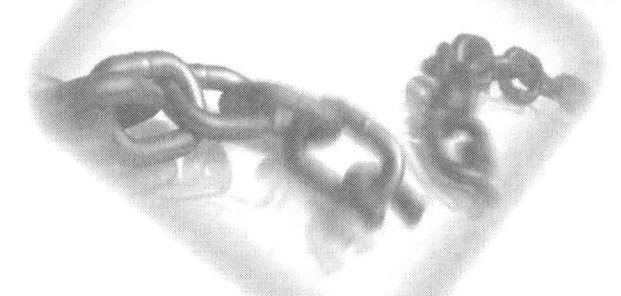

We began our deliverance ministry on Oct. 31st, 1999. At that time we were church counselors. People would call the church and ask to be put on the list for an appointment with us for counseling. We met several times with the counselees. If it was a married couple then we would meet with each one individually, and then the last session we would meet with them together. What would happen many times because of work schedules, or illnesses or other situations that came up, is that we would have to cancel their appointment and re-schedule. Therefore it could take months to meet with people. The Lord began to speak to us that He was doing a new thing in and through us, and what we were doing, would not work for where He was taking us. Therefore, we began to seek Him as to what He would have us do differently. The Lord began to speak to us about doing deliverance quicker. We didn't really understand how this would happen or what we were to do. We received several prophetic words at conferences that God was birthing in us a new thing. He was going to shoot us into deliverance ministry like a rocket, and that is what happened.

Peter and Doris Wagner of Global Harvest Ministries in Colorado Springs, Colorado held a conference on deliverance. It was the first ever world Congress on deliverance and our church, Christian International Family Church, sent us to the conference. We were asked to be on the ministry team to help with personal deliverance. It was at this conference that we saw how deliverance working with the prophetic could be a very valuable tool. When the people came into the room for ministry at the conference, the word of knowledge flowed and the keys to set them free were given by the Holy Spirit. The Lord began to show us how we could implement this into our local church.

When my husband and I returned home from the conference we met with our pastors, Tom and Jane Hamon. We shared the vision that the Lord had given us along with the prophetic words we had received. They felt that we had heard from the Lord. They gave us permission to train up deliverance and healing teams. We launched our teams on October 31st, 1999 at our School of the Holy Spirit. It was an incredible night as hundreds were set free, and healed in their bodies. After about a year we began to travel to other churches training teams. We also began to teach at Christian International's Ministers Training College (MTC) and also at Christian International's Apostolic Prophetic Training conferences. We teach the prophetic healing and deliverance module. We have not only taught and activated thousands in this ministry of deliverance, but we have also delivered and set free thousands of people all over the world; even in various denominations such as the Catholic Church and the Baptist Church in England.

How do we begin the process of delivering people? To cast out demons, you have to call them by their name. Demons have proper names and functional names. An example of a proper name would be Leviathan which is found in many different Scriptures throughout the Bible. Psalms 74:13-14, *"He divided the sea by your strength; you broke the heads of the sea serpents in the waters. ¹⁴You broke the heads of Leviathan in pieces, and gave him his food to the people inhabiting the wilderness.* Isaiah 27:1, *"In that day the Lord with a severe sword, great and strong. Will punish Leviathan, the fleeting serpent. Leviathan that twisted serpent; and he will slay the reptile that is in the sea."* Another proper name would be Belial, found in 2 Corinthians 6:15, *"and what accord has Christ with Belial? Or what part has a believer with an unbeliever?"* Belial in Hebrew, worthless, unprofitableness. Since Satan is opposed to God, antichrist to Christ, Belial being here opposed to Christ, must denote all anti-Christian uncleanness. This is only an example of some of their names.

Next we have functional names, and that would be fear, rejection, shame, loneliness, rebellion, and infirmity, to name a few. It describes the function of the demon. Demons know their name. For example, if you call my name Sharon, I would respond. Demons do the same. When casting demons out, we call them by name. Most of the deliverance done today will be calling the demons out by their function; what they do to the person and how they influence the person. We have had people ask us to have a list of demons. We do not, because I feel that if we have a list of demons then we will get into doing a formula instead of doing it by the spirit. I remember when we went to the conference at the World Prayer Center that Peter and Doris Wagner held and I had forgotten my list of demons. We had been trained to call the demons out by going through a list that was from A-Z with the names of demons on it alphabetically. My thought was oh no, what will I do, I don't have the list on me. This was a setup from the Lord. At this conference, the attendees were offered personal deliverance. We were one of the teams ministering to them. So the first few people that we ministered to sat in the chair and we asked them why they were there. They began to tell us all the reasons that they thought they were there and what they were going through. But, I discerned it was something different. The people would go on and on about their feelings and their emotions. This took a lot of time. The school shootings at Columbine had just happened and many of the people we were ministering to had some relationship with the students that were killed, or to the school. They were parents, teachers and pastors. Three thousand people attended this conference, so we had hundreds of people to minister to. I thought to myself, there is no way we will be able to minister to everybody that is waiting outside this door for us. I hated to even take a bathroom break as the people waiting to come into the room would look at you with a look that said, "Can you minister to me now?"

When the next person came into the room and sat down the Lord spoke to me and said, why don't you move in your gifts? I said well, that's a thought. So I said to the young lady, "We are with a ministry that teaches us to flow in the gifts and hear the voice of God." So how about instead of you telling us why you are here we will ask the Lord and have Him show us. She said that sounded good. So immediately I saw a vision of a city. At that time I had not traveled to the nations, so I did not recognize the city. I said, I see a city, then I stalled a little, because I didn't know what to say. And in my mind I said Lord, you need to help me with this. And the Lord wrote Mexico City over the vision I was seeing. So I said it was Mexico City. The young lady sat up in her chair, and said, "My parents are in Mexico City." I also didn't have a lot of knowledge about territorial spirits or witchcraft. I then began to see a sun in the sky, and people bowing down to it. I shared what I was seeing with the girl. She said it was the sun god RA, and her parents worshiped it. I then began to see how the demons visited her during the night, in her dreams and tormented her. So I began to cast out all the spirits that the Lord was showing me. And we filled her back up with peace, joy, wholeness and life. We also prayed over her sleep that when she lay down her sleep would be sweet. Psalm 4:8, *"I will both lie down in peace, and sleep for you alone, oh Lord make me dwell in safety."* In fifteen minutes, this young lady was set free from generational curses of witchcraft and idolatry. No longer was she tormented with sickness and infirmity. The Lord did a complete work.

We believe when we minister to someone that we should break off the legal territory that the demon has had in the person's life. We feel there can be legal territory for the demonic to stay. So just like in a court of law, if the attorney has evidence against you such as in a contract, then it is legal. We know the enemy is a legalist. The first being unforgiveness and the second is generational curses. We will cover these more fully in the coming chapters of this book. Also at the end of the book we have included the prayers that we use to break off generational curses and to close the door to unforgiveness.

We always begin the deliverance session by pleading the blood of Jesus over them and their family, over ourselves and our families and anything that belongs to us. We then ask for the Holy Spirit to come and be in charge of the Ministry. We stir up the gifts of the word of knowledge and discerning of spirits. In ministering deliverance, there should always be a team of two. Jesus sent them out two by two, not one by one. We don't want to let the enemy have any place. We encourage pastors never to meet with the person alone. There have been many ministries sued because false accusations were made. And if there is only one person it is your word against theirs. We don't say that this will stop lawsuits from ever happening because the enemy hates deliverance, and he would even use other Christians to come against us. We have pastor friends that were taken to court, and even though they won the lawsuit it took years and lots of finances; they lost a lot. We have to have wisdom when ministering. Don't let the enemy set you up for a fall.

So we start the ministry by asking them if they need to forgive anyone, because unforgiveness will hold the demons in place, and it is legal territory for them to stay. Then we break off generational curses that have entered in through the family line. This is the other legal territory. Once this is done, there isn't a demon in hell that can stay.

Next we begin the actual casting out by asking them to keep their eyes open. The reason we ask them to keep their eyes open is because the eyes are the window gate to the soul. Also by looking at the eyes, you can discern what is happening. Matthew 6:22 says, *"the lamp of the body is the eye. If therefore your eye is good your whole body will be full of light."*

We ask them to speak in English, not tongues, because we want to know what is going on. We then tell the person that demons are breath associated. When they come out, it is through the breath functions. So we ask them, as we begin to call out the demons, to blow them out, or as Derek Prince[2] teaches, to cough them out. They can also come out by other breath functions such as burping and yawning. We always joke with the person and tell them we won't think they are being rude if they burp or yawn.

We then begin to pray in the Holy Spirit, stirring up the gifts that are within, *"Therefore, I remind you to stir up the gift of God, which is in you through the laying on of my hands"* (2 Tim. 1:6). We say "Lord; stir up the word of knowledge and the discerning of spirits to a higher level. You know everything that binds and torments this person. More than they want to be free, and we want to see them free, you paid the price to do it. Holy Spirit, you be in charge." Then I pray to bind up excessive manifestations. And we speak to the demons, and I say "you are forbidden to manifest, or cause discomfort, or put on a show, and when I call you out by name, you will go." Luke 4:34-35, says, *"let us alone! What have we to do with you, Jesus of Nazareth? Did you come to destroy us? I know who you are – the holy one of God!" 35But Jesus rebuked him, saying, "be quiet and come out of him!"*

After the casting out is complete, and we feel that the Holy Spirit is saying they are free, we pray over their five senses. The five senses, or the five gates as we call them, are the sense of smell, eye gate, ear gate, sense of taste, and touch. We have found out through the years that we need

---
[2] Derek Prince (1915-2003); International Bible teacher who was well known for his teachings about demons.

to speak a healing to these five areas. When people see someone that reminds them of the person that abused or abandoned them it can be an entry point. If they have looked at pornography, it can pollute their mind for a long time. A smell can remind them of what the person smelled like that abused them. This is just another key the Lord has shown us to use as we deliver the person.

Then we fill them up by having them drink in a fresh infilling of the Holy Spirit and imparting the opposite of what was cast out. If we cast out death, we impart life. If we cast out fear, then we impart peace. Doubt and unbelief, then we impart faith.

We seal the deliverance by saying "I seal the deliverance in the name of Jesus and no demon can steal what God has just done." We then end the session by spending time to thank the Lord for what he has just done.

The last thing we do is clean out the room spiritually. We say everything that was just cast out of this person and tell them to go where Jesus would send you. We have had teachings on sending the demons to the dry places, the sea, and the abyss. Yet we feel you can't go wrong if you say, "We send you demons to where Jesus sends you."

Here are two recent testimonies of flowing prophetically and setting people free.

> Dear Bob/Sharon,
>
> I want to start by saying that you guys are a blessing for Christian International and to all the ones that have the privilege to have Christian International as coverage. I really respect what you guys do by putting God's call first, with compassion to others, even sacrificing personal things like time, plans,

energy, and finances.

Don't ever think that the body of Christ doesn't notice the efforts you guys do, that is why I wanted to stop to thank you first for the big blessing you guys are leaving behind. Definitely you guys are making the Father proud.

I want to share all that I went through in my deliverance with the idea that I was going to be free from generational curses and things like that, but I had a pain in my back from almost a year and a half ago. One day I went to exercise and I noticed that at the end of my routine I started with a pain in my back that went from my neck all the way down to my lower back. I didn't pay too much attention to the pain but over the months it was growing little by little and becoming sharper to the point that sometimes I had unpleasant days that started having an impact on my character. And even when most of the time I was not complaining about it; other people were paying the consequences of my discomfort, like my employees, and my wife.

This reminded me of the plague in Exodus 8:8-9 referring to the frogs. We are sometimes like Pharaoh. We are disgusted with the frogs but we learn to live with them. We get so familiar with the frogs to the point when Moses asked Pharaoh to let him know when to pray about the frogs to remove them.

Pharaoh's response was with the frogs to the point that when Moses asked Pharaoh to let him know when to pray for him to remove all the frogs from his life, to my surprise Pharaoh responded, okay do it but... tomorrow... I thought he was disgusted with the frogs and he couldn't take it anymore. When we get like that we start complaining a little bit first but then we start getting use to it and allow the devil to torment us, and little by little we let him get to all areas of our lives giving up our freedoms to him, and when we realize something is not right, he is already controlling even our daily joy. What is worse is being sons of a powerful father that can set us free from all our afflictions and torments on the spot but we are not claiming our rights...!

When these precious ministers prayed for me, the second thing that GOD revealed to Prophet Sharon was the pain that ran from my neck to my knees; on the spot, I was free, I didn't feel anything until when I went to sit in another seat and felt nothing I was so use to it that I started looking for it and couldn't find it. It was gone and until this day is gone... all the glory to our FATHER. Thank GOD for mature Christians that can share their blessings... we'll be looking for another visit soon!

Love you guys,
Saul Reyes

Next Testimony:

P. Sharon, as I was testifying to you, I was overwhelmed with the power of GOD. On that Saturday that we were activated in the prophetic deliverance I was able to realize the power that is in us. My wife and I had encounters with demons before and saw them being manifested in other people. We fought to cast them out and the problem was that they always put on a Hollywood show, as you called it. Screaming, twisting around on the floor, shaking, vomiting and on and on and on; you know how the demons do. But as you said, the good thing now is that through the equipping that you passed on to us and now that we know and understand the power and authority that was placed in us at the moment we allowed JESUS into our lives and how the gifts of the spirit are stirred up in us at the moment we started to do the deliverance; if people would understand the power that WE THE CHURCH HAVE we wouldn't (the church) have so much of a struggle. We would stand our ground and keep fighting for what belongs to us, so please keep doing the great job that GOD has called you to do. It is a blessing to have met you and your husband, Apostle Bob, give my regards to him and hopefully we will see you again soon.

Henry & Charo Garcia, Ft. Lauderdale, Florida

I shared these testimonies to give you an understanding of how this works. We had never met these people before but the Lord met their needs and set them free. We have so many testimonies of the same thing happening all over the world as we train and minister.

34Your Passport To Freedom

Chapter 4
Forgiveness: A Key to Deliverance

Forgiveness is unconditional and God requires it. *"For if you forgive men their trespasses, your heavenly father will also forgive you: but if he forgives not men their trespasses, neither will your Father forgive your trespasses"* (Matt. 6:14-15).

Luke 6:37, It says *"Forgive and you will be forgiven."* It is not hard to see where God stands on this issue. When people say they do not feel like forgiving, we tell them it isn't an emotion, but a decision. It is an act of their will. Therefore, if we want to be forgiven, we must forgive.

Webster's dictionary defines forgive as:

    1. To grant pardon for or remission of something.

    2. To cease to blame for, feel resentment against.

    3. To show forgiveness. Absolve, excuse or exonerate.

The New International study Bible defines forgiveness as:

    1. Pardon and release from penalty for wrongdoing.

    2. God's delivery from sin's wages. (Rom. 6:23)

3. The Christian act of freeing from guilt and blame those by whom one has suffered wrong.
(Matt. 6:14; Col. 3:13)

The reason a person must forgive is because it ties them in bondage to the one they have not forgiven. In addition, it gives the devil and his demons the legal grounds to keep them in bondage. This is the first legal ground we take back from the enemy when taking someone through deliverance, to make sure they forgive those that have hurt them in any way.

Matthew 18:34-35, *"And his master was angry, and delivered him to the torturers until you should pay all of that was due to him. *³⁵*"So my heavenly father also will do to you, if each of you, from his heart, does not forgive his brother his trespasses."* From this Scripture we see that the Lord will turn us over to the torturers. Some versions of the Bible call them "tormentors." Does that sound like demons to you? So we are unable to set people free unless they forgive.

If they are not willing to do this, we may cancel the ministry appointment until such time as they can forgive. This is necessary because the person receiving Ministry will be in more bondage after we pray for them than before we pray for them. Luke 11:24-26, *"When an unclean spirit goes out of a man, he goes through dry places, seeking rest; and finding none, he says, "I will return to my house from which I came."* ²⁵*And when he comes, he finds it swept and put in order.* ²⁶*"Then he goes and takes with him seven other spirits more wicked than himself, and they enter and dwell there; and the last state of that man is worse than the first."*

Dr. Bill Hamon (founder of Christian International Ministries) says that demons are like buzzards: if they have nothing to feed on like unforgiveness, they will leave. This is so true. If we take away that legal territory from the demons they leave.

Not only do we have to forgive others, but sometimes we have to forgive ourselves, which can be hard. We've seen this many times with individuals; they find it very easy to forgive others, but don't have the same grace for themselves. We may blame ourselves for wrong choices or allowing ourselves to become victims.

It may even be God that we have to forgive. I know for myself, I really blamed God for some of the things that happened in my life. I thought He's God, and He could have intervened, and not allowed things to happen. But I also had a fear of the Lord. I am not talking about having a Godly fear or reverence, I'm talking about fearing that God would just let you die if you didn't measure up, if you didn't do enough, or if you got Him mad. I remember when I was little there were some men working on our farm, they were cutting trees down in the woods. My mom looked out the window and said, "Those men are breaking the Sabbath, God just might kill them for that." I remember watching out the window to see if He would do it. So, that is the way I perceived God to be. To even allow myself to say that I had unforgiveness toward him scared me. But the truth was that I did. So when I got a revelation and realized he really wasn't like that I let all the judgment and unforgiveness go. The Lord seems to get the blame most of the time for what the devil does.

Forgiveness is not an emotion. It is a decision of the will. This is where people have a problem. They think they have to feel like forgiving the person. What we have found is that when someone makes a conscious effort to forgive; the emotions will line up. Just like fear has torment, unforgiveness has torment too. The enemy will have us rehearse and rehearse all the wrong that was done to us. I was teaching my deliverance class in California, and at the end of the teaching, I ministered deliverance to the class. I started by delivering a few people to show how it is done. Then I used those people to help minister to the others. I teach and activate at the same time. I called this lady up to minister to her, and as I was calling the demons out they didn't seem to want to go. The Lord spoke to me that she had unforgiveness toward someone. So I asked her if she had forgiven those who she needed to forgive. Her response to me was that "You don't know what they did to me." I told her that by forgiving them, it didn't mean what they did was right. All it was doing was bringing her torment. Most of the time the people who caused the pain don't even remember what they did. They go on with their life, and here we are stuck feeling the same way we did when the event happened. The devil continues to torment our mind with that memory. But the answer is simple; the freedom comes when we release them to the Lord. Sometimes we might need to tell the Lord about it. Not in a "poor me" way. Psalm 142:1-2, *"I cry out to the Lord with my voice; with my voice to the Lord I make my supplication. ²I pour out my complaint before Him; I declare before Him my trouble."* There might be times when we just need to talk to the Lord about it. But there can be a danger of staying in that emotion too long and letting self-pity take over. For the most part, we just need to forgive, and when we forgive, the emotions can be healed and the memory of all that happened. As I said, when you cast out the demons after forgiveness has taken place then the torment goes too.

Blame keeps wounds open; only forgiveness heals. Emotional healing is not the only part of us that forgiveness affects. It can also produce physical healing. There have been many studies that have looked at the role of forgiveness in health.

At the University of Wisconsin, researchers ran a study on thirty-six male veterans with coronary artery disease – each person was still dealing with a painful emotional problem. Some were war related, some childhood memories, some domestic issues, and some work related.

Part of the group underwent ten weeks of forgiveness training, while the others did not. The researchers found that those trained in forgiveness showed improved blood flow to the heart compared to those men who had not gone through the forgiveness training.

While there are some controversies in the secular world over forgiveness affecting our physical health, the John Templeton foundation in Radner, Pennsylvania, has given millions of dollars toward grants for forgiveness research; both toward forgiving others and ourselves.

It has been shown that unforgiving people have increased anxiety symptoms, paranoia, psychosomatic problems, heart disease, and are less resistant to physical illness. Unforgiveness also affects the auto-immune system. Think about it, when we become angry with someone, doesn't that raise our blood pressure? Many times, when trying to minister deliverance to someone who is sick, we find that unforgiveness is what has held the infirmity in place. We were ministering in London, England and a lady named Angela had her ear healed because she forgave her husband. Here is her testimony.

> For the past ten years, I have been a single parent with three children and I was angry with the Father of my children for not giving any money toward their upkeep. During a meeting at Tower of Faith Centre I had pain in my right ear. I phoned a doctor for an appointment on that Friday, February 22. During the service on Saturday, February 23, Prophetess Sharon Parkes led us in a prayer of forgiveness and I forgave him. Immediately after the prayer, my ear was healed.

Chapter 5
Understanding Generational Curses

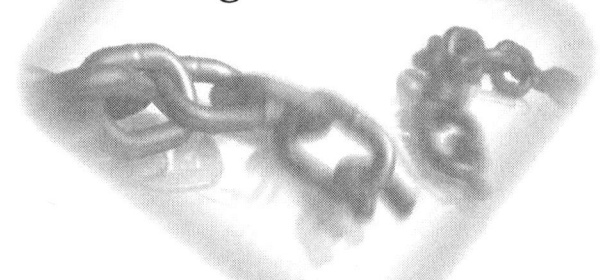

The Bible shows there is something called iniquity or generational curses that can be passed down through our family for three to four generations. Exodus 20:5 says, *"you shall not bow down to them nor serve them. For I, the Lord your God, am a jealous God, visiting the iniquity of the fathers upon the children to the third and fourth generations of those that hate Me."* Deuteronomy 5:9 and Lamentations 5:7, *"Our fathers sinned and are no more, but we bear their iniquities."* Many Christians are caught in an endless cycle of sinning and repenting. They are trying to serve the Lord, but there is something there that tries to get them to fall back into sin. The sin could be addictions, unforgiveness, lying, gossip, or worry instead of faith. Before when we ministered to people in our church, there were cycles in these people's lives that they kept falling into. I would become very frustrated with them. I couldn't understand why they couldn't stop doing what they were doing. Once I found out about generational curses I began to understand why they couldn't break free and stop sinning.

When our ancestors sin, that brings a generational curse upon us. It doesn't just go to the grave with them when they die. The following Scripture confirms that.

Numbers 14:18, *"The Lord is long-suffering and abundant in mercy, forgiving iniquity and transgression; but He by no means clears the guilty, visiting the iniquity of the fathers on the children to the third and fourth generation."*

In Romans 7:15-17 Paul is making a statement that he doesn't understand what he is doing. And even says he hates what he does. He wants to do good, and not sin, but he keeps doing it. It almost sounds like Paul is double-minded. But when you read it, you can see there is a force that is holding Paul captive, and he is not able to be free and make the right choices.

We all know that the devil is a legalist, and he uses legal territory to afflict us. When we become born-again, our eternal life is changed. When we die we will go to heaven. When we break off generational curses from our lives, this affects our quality of life. When Jesus died on the cross, he purchased for us a quality of life. John 10:10 says *it is an abundant life.* And I want that quality of life. Too many of us are just getting by; putting up with everything the devil throws our way. That's why I enjoy teaching on generational curses and bringing a revelation to people that just breaking off these curses will bring such freedom. So many people argue that we can't have a generational curse, yet we see it in many families. Whether it's poverty, premature death, or infirmity; people just can't seem to get ahead. Even the medical field recognizes these generational curses. When you go to the doctor he gives you a paper to fill out which asks if there are heart problems, asthma, cancer, diabetes or lung disease in your family. They ask you to put a check beside all that applies to your family. Is this not a curse to have these diseases and infirmities? If the doctor recognizes that we get these diseases, passed down from our family, then it must be medically proven. Are we not Christians and yet we are getting diseases passed down to us from our ancestors. Sickness is not a blessing, it is a curse.

The Hebrew word for iniquity is **Avon** (Aw Vone) it means to blame, evil, perversion. It comes from the root word **Avah** (Aw Vaw) meaning to bend or to distort, to crook, pervert, trouble, do wickedly, do wrong, bow down. The root of **Aw-Vaw is Chata (Khaw-Taw)** it means to miss or to sin.

If we cast out the demonic and do not break off generational curses first, the demons have a right to come back, because we have not taken away the legal territory that they have to be there.

We have also seen that generational curses stop us from receiving healing. Psalms 31:10, *"For my life is spent with grief, And my years with signing; My strength fails because of my iniquity, And my bones waste away."*

I always say that this sounds like osteoporosis. Isn't the meaning of osteoporosis bones wasting away? So this could be an open door to that happening to us, if generational curses have not been broken off. Many people are not able to receive breakthrough of healing in their body because of generational curses not being dealt with. After they are broken off, and the hindrance removed, then they receive their total healing. Generational curses/iniquity, keeps us from receiving all that God has for us, personally, physically, spiritually and financially. David wrote in Psalms 66:18, *"If I regard iniquity in my heart, the Lord will not hear."* Jeremiah 5:25 says, *"Your iniquities have turned these things away, and your sins have withheld good from you."*

We always give the modern example of generational curses, as seen in the Kennedy family. We see many of the Kennedys have died prematurely. They have been caught up in addictions and lust.

In the Bible we see the pattern of generational curses. I use King David for a lot of my teachings. This is a man after God's own heart, but yet he dealt with a lot of issues. Look at 2 Samuel 11:2-27. In these Scriptures we see that King David had a weakness toward sexual sin and lust. If we look in Matthew chapter 1:5 we see that David is descended from Rahab, who is also known as Rahab the harlot. So this would definitely open David up to a generational curse of lust to be passed down to him. We can see how it affected him. David entered into lust, adultery, deception, conspiracy, and murder. David, by giving in to the generational curse, has now opened his family up to the same curse being passed down, growing each time. Once the generational curse is yielded to, it grows. I call it the snowball effect. For those who have grown up around snow, and have made a snowman, we start by forming a snowball. Then we put that snowball either on the ground or on a hill. As we began to roll it on the ground or let it roll down the hill that snowball gathers more snow and becomes bigger and bigger. That is how generational curses work. If they are given into, then they grow in strength as they are passed down to the next generation. So David passed down generational curses to his sons, Amnon and Absalom.

In 2 Samuel 13 Amnon rapes Tamar and her brother Absalom murders Amnon for it. So you see, Amnon lusted after Tamar and then gave in to it. Much like David did with Bathsheba. Then Absalom commits murder, just like his father David did with Uriah, Bathsheba's husband. Although David didn't actually pull the trigger to murder Uriah, he had him sent to the forefront of the battle, where he knew he would be killed.

David had another son, his name was Solomon. Let's see if we see any generational curses, especially of lust in Solomon. Look at 1 Kings 11:1-11. Here are verses 3-4, *"And he had seven hundred wives, princesses, and three hundred concubines and his wives turned away his heart. ⁴For it was so, when Solomon was old, that his wives turned his heart after other gods, and his heart was not loyal to the Lord his God, as was the heart of his father David."* In these Scriptures we see that Solomon had a strong spirit of lust. My husband always says to do the math. Seven hundred plus three hundred equals a thousand women. I would say that yes, he had a strong spirit of lust. What really showed me how strong generational curses are was in verse nine, where it says that the Lord God of Israel, had appeared to him twice. The other reference for this is found in 1 Kings 9:2-9 the Lord appeared to Solomon two times, saying to Solomon, if you go after these foreign women, they will turn your heart away from me.

Think of it, what would you do, if the Lord appeared to you twice and said don't do this? Do you think you would listen? We only have to think that God is going to appear to us and we would be on our face repenting. When I was studying generational curses, and I saw these Scriptures, I really understood the power they have over us. I began to have more compassion for people that have wanted to change their lives and break out of sin but couldn't. Now, we had the key to help them.

The Lord has shown us how we can break off generational curses and release generational blessings. First of all, we repent of the sins of our fathers. It always starts with repentance. And we asked the Lord to forgive them, and by doing this it closes the door to those familiar spirits. I want to share a vision the Lord gave me about generational curses. I saw the person that we were ministering to walking down a long hallway or corridor. It was lined with doors on both sides. As the person we were ministering to walked down this hallway, they would stop by the doors. The doors on both sides of them would open up and demons would reach out and torment them. As they continued down the hallway, this would keep happening, with the demons reaching out and tormenting them. I asked the Lord what this vision meant and he said that these were generational curses tormenting the person through their walk of life. He said to tell those we were ministering to, to see his hand on the doors closing them, and that they would not be opened up any more because he had closed the door to the generational curses. I always share this vision because it shows people that the Lord can and will set us free from generational curses.

The prayer for generational curses and how to minister to this area is in chapter 9. We have seen thousands and thousands of people set free when we break off these family curses. A lot of the curses come down through Freemasonry, which will be covered in the next chapter.

Chapter 6
What is Freemasonry?

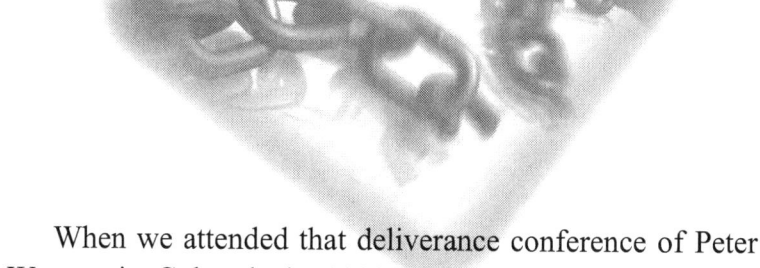

When we attended that deliverance conference of Peter Wagner in Colorado in 1999 many of the speakers were teaching on "Freemasonry." Up until then, my husband Bob and I knew very little about Freemasonry. There was a minister from New Zealand, Dr. Selwyn Stevens, who was one of the guest speakers at this conference. He brought great revelation about it.

We have found out that many in the body of Christ don't know much about Freemasonry. We have seen in our ministry much healing come when we minister freedom from Freemasonry. So the question is; who are the Freemasons?

Freemasonry, as it is known today was established in London, England in the early 1700s. Freemasons are members of the free and ancient order of Masons. There is some evidence that the first lodge was established in Scotland in the 1600s. But the first United Grand Lodge was formed at the Goose and Gridiron Tavern in London, England. Some even say that Freemasonry was established hundreds of years earlier. But what I can say for sure is that Freemasons bring a curse on themselves, their families and their churches. This is stated in many books that expose Freemasonry, but we have seen it ourselves, especially in the area of infirmity.

We also know that Freemasonry is a secret society with many rituals. A few years ago my husband Bob was teaching at a conference held in Santa Maria, California. He was teaching on exposing Freemasonry. One of the things he said that night was that Freemasonry was a secret society. That was on a Wednesday night. In Saturday's paper of the *Santa Maria Times* the headline read "Freemasonry, we are not a secret society, but we are a society with secrets." You guessed it; there must have been a free mason at that meeting. The article went on to say they were just a group of men who met together for companionship, and also that they helped the community in many ways. Most men when they join freemasonry only go up the first three degrees. And most of them do not realize what is behind Freemasonry. There are many different offshoots of Freemasonry. The first three degrees are known as the blue lodge. Many oaths are taken and spoken during this initiation of the first three degrees. The Bible is very clear that Christians are not to swear oaths. Matthew 5:33-34 says, *Jesus forbids Oaths "Again you have heard that it was said to those of old, 'You shall not swear falsely, but shall perform your oaths to the Lord.' [34]But I say to you, do not swear at all: neither by heaven, for it is God's throne."*

Freemasonry is a secret society attended by men, and they go to their meetings at the lodges without telling their wives. We have heard of marriages breaking up due to fear and secrecy as the husbands attend meetings and don't tell their wives. The wives have no idea what their husbands are doing. Husbands and wives should not have secrets from one another. This causes separation and division, even in the spiritual area.

Freemasons are alive and well in many churches today. Many are pastors, elders and deacons, along with church members. We have personally seen on bumpers of cars, and license plates of ministers, the free masonry logo. You can go online and find the different logos that they use. This way, you will be familiar with the Freemason logo and be able to spot it.

Freemasonry claims to be a religion. But is it a Christian religion? They would like you to believe it is. But you will find that Freemasons come from all religious backgrounds. Some are Buddhist, Muslims, Hindus and Christians. So if Freemasonry was a Christian institution then the Buddhists, Muslims and the other cults could not conscientiously belong. Freemasonry leads people to believe that all gods are equal, when in fact, the Bible is very clear. In John 14:6 Jesus said to him, *"I am the way, the truth, and the life. No one comes to the Father except through Me."* In Freemasonry they say the Bible is a sacred writing, but only a few carefully selected passages are used so as not to offend members of non-Christian faith and to support the Masonic mythological beliefs. Some of the Bible references they use are the ones that relate to the building of Solomon's Temple.

A Past Master of a Chicago Lodge, Edmond Ronayne, wrote this in his book called *Masters Carpet*. "All my experience in and out of Masonic lodges has gone to establish the fact in my mind that Freemasonry, in all its departments, is the most corrupt and wicked, and contains the greatest amount of falsehood of any other institution on the face of the globe. It is positively and absolutely selfish in every single element of its pagan composition, and can truthfully lay no more claim to charity, benevolence or goodness of any other name or description than could say, the heathen organizations, which Christian civilization has long been banished from the world." As you see from this excerpt from Ronayne that most of the information we get about Freemasons are from former Masons, not from an outside source.

We made the statement that most Freemasons only reach the first three degrees. The central religious deity, who claims the worship of Gentile, Hindu, Buddhist and Christian alike, is carefully hidden from the members. All religious persuasions are encouraged to believe that their particular deity is indeed the one known by the initials T. G. A. O. T. U. The members of the first three degrees to which the highest membership percentage belongs are led to believe that the letters stand for "the grand architect of the universe." So Christians who believe that this deity is Jesus Christ are being deceived into committing idolatry. And these professing Christians are in danger of God's judgment.

Unless a master mason is invited and reaches a higher degree such as the 30th and 32nd degree, he may never learn the real name of the Masonic deity. It isn't until the 32nd degree that they are actually worshiping Lucifer. Many have said England is a possible exception to this rule as special revelation is sometimes made on completing the third degree. So, what this is saying is that about two thirds of the membership is deliberately kept from knowing the truth about who they are worshiping.

You may then be asking yourself how a Christian would want to join Freemasonry. As we said, they are deceived into thinking that this is a Christian organization that does so many good things. The Shriners have a hospital for burn victims, and also for crippled children. These hospitals charge very little if anything for the treatment that is received there. But we know good works don't get you into heaven. I believe that this is just a façade they project so they will not be questioned and their name will be associated with the good works they do.

The Lord allowed me to see how the spread of deception happens with a Freemason. Once when we were on a cruise, we met a man that was a Freemason. I knew he was a Mason because of the Masonic ring on his finger. I commented on his ring. He said that it was a Shriner's ring. I said, so you're a Freemason? He said yes I am. I asked him how he got involved in Freemasonry. He said that he was a schoolteacher, and that one of his students had gotten in a car accident. So he went to visit him at the hospital and he met the student's father and uncle who shared with him about Freemasonry. They invited him to attend a meeting. You must be invited to become a Freemason. You cannot just go to a meeting and join. He said the student's father and uncle were Christians, and so was he. He was really impressed by all the good things that the Masons did. So he accepted their offer to go to the meeting and joined the Masons. That was how he became a Freemason.

I asked the man if he was a Christian. He said yes. I then asked him if it was true that as a Freemason you worship with people who also worship other gods besides Jesus Christ. He replied that it was true and that atheists cannot belong. I spoke again, saying that you as a Christian worship with people that deny the deity of Jesus Christ. He replied once again with, "Yes, as I told you atheists cannot belong. You must have a higher deity." Then I realized the deception that was over his mind. It was as if the demon had closed his eyes, ears and mind to the truth behind Freemasonry. I saw how strong the deception was over this man. He was professing to be a believer of Christ, but yet participating in pagan rituals. That is why we bind up and break off the spirit of deception from people after getting rid of the spirit of Freemasonry.

I want to focus on the founding fathers of the United States. In the writing of the Declaration of Independence, fifty-six men signed it. Nine were known Masons. Of the officers of the Continental Army, thirty-three out of seventy-four were Masons. George Washington and all of his generals were Freemasons. He was also the first president of the United States. The all seeing, third eye of Freemasonry is on the back of the one dollar bill. It has been said that the Horus or all seeing third eye is watching over our money. I believe there is truth behind that because Freemasons are very involved in the financial arena. In the United States, there are very influential people who are in Freemasonry, some very well known business and governmental people. My husband Bob makes the comment that how can we say that we are founded as a Christian nation when in our foundation, is Freemasonry.

There's been much repentance and prayer over the Freemasonry involvement in our nation and government. When George W. Bush was sworn into office, it was a rainy, snowy and cold day in Washington D.C. He was not sworn into office on the Masonic Bible, which had been done for hundreds of years. And Masons did not want their Bible, which dated back to George Washington, to be destroyed or ruined by the weather. This was an answer to prayer for the intercessors who had been praying for the Masonic curse to be broken off of our country.

This is a list of presidents of the United States who were and are Freemasons.

1. George Washington
2. James Monroe
3. Andrew Jackson
4. James Polk
5. James Buchanan
6. Andrew Johnson
7. James Garfield
8. William McKinley
9. Theodore Roosevelt
10. Howard Taft
11. Warren Harding
12. Franklin Roosevelt
13. Harry Truman
14. Gerald Ford
15. Ronald Reagan
16. Jimmy Carter
17. George Bush, Sr.

George W. Bush was supposedly not a Freemason, but he was a member of the skull and bones in college, which is an offshoot of Freemasonry. Abraham Lincoln was not a Freemason, but he did apply for membership in a lodge then withdrew his application because he didn't want people to think he was applying to the lodge to get votes.

Charles Finney wrote in his book *Character, Claims and Practical Workings of Freemasonry* that "God holds the church in every branch of it, responsible for its opinions and actions in accordance with the light, which, in his providence, is afforded them. If any particular branch of the church has better means of information, and therefore light on moral questions than another branch, its responsibility is greater in proportion to its greater means of information."

"While masonry was a secret, the church has no light and no responsibility respecting it. Although individual members of the church were Freemasons, as a body, she knew nothing of masonry; therefore she could say nothing. But the state of the case is now greatly changed. Freemasonry is now revealed. It is no longer a secret to any who wish to be informed. Now since these revelations are made, both the church and the world are aware of what masonry really is. God demands and the world has a right to expect that the church will take new action and very truthful testimony in respect to this situation. She cannot now innocently hold her peace. The light has come." He also said "the church is required to speak out and take action to reveal the church's views on compatibility or incompatibility of Freemasonry with the Christian religion."[3]

We personally know of churches splitting up when we brought out the truth of Freemasonry. Freemasons will try to control and manipulate the church. One church found out that a few of the members were Freemasons. They asked them to resign. Instead, they left the church and took their

---

[3] Charles Finney, *Character, Claims and Practical Workings of Freemasonry,* taken from chapter 19 titled "Relations of Masonry to The Church of Christ."

finances with them. They gave large tithes to the church, but after our teaching the pastor learned of the curses that they brought with them so he wanted no part of it.

Finney was asked what should be done with a great number of professed Christians who are Freemasons. His answer was to let them have no more to do with it. He stated that Christian men should labor with them, plead with them, and endeavor to make them see it to be their duty to abandon it. To the continuing Freemason, he said they should not be allowed a place in the church.

So, what Finney is saying is that we as a church have a duty to expose the truth about Freemasonry. There have been studies that have shown Freemasonry has an influence on stopping revival. Just like we say that deliverance is the booster rocket to revival, we feel when we deal with Freemasonry the church will grow and flourish.

In our ministry, when we deal with Freemasonry, we have seen immediate deliverance for people. There was deliverance from financial failure, marriage problems, and infirmity. Here is one such testimony.

> I am very excited to be giving you my testimony of what God has recently done through your ministry. For years I have struggled with severe sinus and allergy problems; I truly believed that I would continue taking allergy medicine my entire life. Well that was until I took your prophetic healing and deliverance course this past weekend in Suffolk, Virginia.
>
> When you began to teach about the Freemasons, and how many illnesses have stemmed from this organization, I knew there was a glimmer of hope.

You see my father is a mason.

As we began to read the prayer of release for Freemasonry and their descendants, renouncing all ties and associations with them, I began to feel drainage in my sinus cavity, almost as if someone had physically taking their hands off of my nose and face. I am convinced that from that moment on, I was healed, set free, and delivered from all sinus and allergy problems! Praise God!

In addition, as I have become delivered and set free, I desire to see others set free too. I called my brother up, who has been recently having bouts with high blood pressure and head pain (at the age of twenty-three), and I told him what I learned from the course. I sent him the prayer of release, and expected him to be set free, instantaneously! Thank you so much for allowing God to use you mightily in the kingdom.

Best regards,
Lakia Gordon, Newport News, Virginia

Once while ministering in Chicago, a pastor was going through the release of Freemasonry prayer, and she was immediately healed of sinusitis and allergies. She shared with us later that both sets of her grandparents were Freemasons, and that she had had sinusitis and allergy problems for over twenty years. But as she said the prayer, she was instantly healed.

Going through the prayer of release of Freemasonry is similar to the breaking of generational curses prayer. It breaks the covenant that our ancestors or we may have made with the enemy. It releases us from all the curses that have been passed on to us.

What is Freemasonry?   57

The author of the following prayer is Dr. Selwyn Stevens from Wellington, New Zealand. His ministry is called Jubilee International and you can find this prayer on his website.[4]

PRAYER OF RELEASE FOR FREEMASONS & THEIR DESCENDANTS

If you were once a member of a Masonic organization or are a descendant of someone who was, we recommend that you pray through this prayer from you heart. Please don't be like the Masons who are given their obligations and oaths one line at a time and without prior knowledge of the requirements. Please read it through first so you know what is involved. It is best to pray this aloud with a Christian witness present. We suggest a brief pause following each paragraph to allow the Holy Spirit to show any related issues which may require attention.

A significant number of people also reported having experienced physical and spiritual healings as diverse as long-term headaches and epilepsy as the result of praying through this prayer. Christian counselors and pastors in many countries have been using this prayer in counseling situations and seminars for several years, with real and significant results.

There are differences between British Commonwealth Masonry and American & Prince Hall Masonry in the higher degrees. Degrees unique to Americans are marked with three stars at the beginning of each paragraph. Those of British & Commonwealth decent shouldn't need to pray through those paragraphs.

> Father God, creator of heaven and earth, I come to you in the name of Jesus Christ your Son. I come as a sinner seeking forgiveness and cleansing from all sins committed against you, and others made in

---
[4] www.jubilee-resources.com.

your image. I honour my earthly father and mother and all of my ancestors of flesh and blood, and of the spirit by adoption and godparents, but I utterly turn away from and renounce all their sins. I forgive all my ancestors for the effects of their sins on me and my children. I confess and renounce all of my own sins. I renounce and rebuke Satan and every spiritual power of his affecting me and my family.

I renounce and forsake all involvement in Freemasonry or any other lodge or craft by my ancestors and myself. In the name of Jesus Christ, I renounce and cut off Witchcraft, the principal spirit behind Freemasonry, and I renounce and cut off Baphomet, the Spirit of Antichrist and the spirits of Death, and Deception. I renounce the insecurity, the love of position and power, the love of money, avarice or greed, and the pride which would have led my ancestors into Masonry. I renounce all the fears which held them in Masonry, especially the fear of death, fears of men, and fears of trusting, in the name of Jesus Christ.

I renounce every position held in the lodge by any of my ancestors or myself, including "Master," "Worshipful Master," or any other. I renounce the calling of any man "Master," for Jesus Christ is my only master and Lord, and He forbids anyone else having that title. I renounce the entrapping of others into Masonry, and observing the helplessness of others during the rituals. I renounce the effects of Masonry passed on to me through any female ancestor who felt distrusted and rejected by her husband as he entered and attended any lodge and refused to tell her of his secret activities. I also renounce all obligations, oaths and curses enacted by every female member of my family through any direct membership of all Women's

Orders of Freemasonry, the Order of the Eastern Star, or any other Masonic or occultic Organization.

Blue Lodge (1st Degree)

In the name of Jesus Christ I renounce the oaths taken and the curses involved in the First or Entered Apprentice Degree, especially their effects on the throat and tongue. I renounce the Hoodwink blindfold and its effects on spirit, emotions and eyes, including all confusion, fear of the dark, fear of the light, and fear of sudden noises. I renounce the blinding of spiritual truth, the darkness of the soul, the false imagination, condescension and the spirit of poverty caused by the ritual of this degree. I also renounce the usurping of the marriage covenant by the removal of the wedding ring. I renounce the secret word, BOAZ, and all it means. I renounce the serpent clasp on the apron, and the spirit of Python which it brought to squeeze the spiritual life out of me. I renounce the ancient pagan teaching from Babylon & Egypt and the symbolism of the First Tracing Board. I renounce the mixing and mingling of truth and error, the mythology, fabrications and lies taught as truth, and the dishonesty by leaders as to the true understanding of the ritual, and the blasphemy of this degree of Freemasonry. I renounce the presentation to every compass direction, for all the Earth is the Lord's, and everything in it.

I renounce the cable tow noose around the neck, the fear of choking and also every spirit causing asthma, hay fever, emphysema or any other breathing difficulty. I renounce the ritual daggers, or the compass point, sword or spear held against the breast, the fear of death by stabbing pain, and the fear of heart attack from this degree, and the absolute secrecy demanded under a witchcraft oath and sealed by kissing the Volume of the Sacred Law. I also renounce kneeling to the false deity known as the Great Architect of the Universe, and humbly ask the One True God to forgive me for this idolatry, in the name of Jesus Christ. I renounce the pride of proven character and good standing required prior to joining Freemasonry, and the resulting self-righteousness of being good enough to stand before God without the need of a saviour. I now pray for healing of... (throat, vocal cords, nasal passages, sinus, bronchial tubes, etc.) for healing of the speech area, and the release of the Word of God to me and through me and my family.

2nd Degree

In the name of Jesus Christ I renounce the oaths taken and the curses involved in the Second or FellowCraft Degree of Masonry, especially the curses on the heart and chest. I renounce the secret ords SHIBBOLETH and JACHIN, and all that these mean. I renounce the ancient pagan teaching and symbolism of the Second Tracing Board. I renounce the Sign of Reverence to the Generative Principle. I cut off emotional hardness, apathy, indifference, unbelief, and deep anger from me and my family. In the name of Jesus Christ I pray for the healing of... (the chest/lung/heart area) and also for the healing of my emotions, and ask to be made sensitive to the Holy Spirit of God.

3rd Degree

In the name of Jesus Christ I renounce the oaths taken and the curses involved in the Third or Master Mason Degree, especially the curses on the stomach and womb area. I renounce the secret words TUBAL CAIN and MAHA BONE, and all that they mean. I renounce the ancient pagan teaching and symbolism of the Third Tracing Board used in the ritual. I renounce the Spirit of Death from the blows to the head enacted as ritual murder, the fear of death, false martyrdom, fear of violent gang attack, assault, or rape, and the helplessness of this degree. I renounce the falling into the coffin or stretcher involved in the ritual of murder. In the name of Jesus Christ I renounce Hiram Abiff, the false saviour of Freemasons revealed in this degree. I renounce the false resurrection of this degree, because only Jesus Christ is the Resurrection and the Life! In the name of Jesus Christ I pray for healing of the... (the stomach, gall bladder, womb, liver, and any other organs of my body affected by Masonry), and I ask for a release of compassion and understanding for me and my family.

I renounce the pagan ritual of the "Point within a Circle" with all its bondages and phallus worship. I renounce the symbol "G" and its veiled pagan symbolism and bondages, I renounce the occultic mysticism of the black and white mosaic chequered floor with the tessellated boarder and five-pointed blazing star.

I renounce the All-Seeing Third Eye of Freemasonry or Horus in the forehead and its pagan and occult symbolism. I now close that Third eye and all occult ability to see into the spiritual realm, in the name of the Lord Jesus Christ, and put my trust in the Holy Spirit sent by Jesus Christ for all I need to know on spiritual matters. I renounce all false communions taken, all mockery of the redemptive work of Jesus Christ on the cross of Calvary, all unbelief, confusion and depression. I renounce and forsake the lie of Freemasonry that man is not sinful, but merely imperfect, and so can redeem himself through good works. I rejoice that the Bible states that I cannot do a single thing to earn my salvation, but that I can only be saved by grace through faith in Jesus Christ and what He accomplished on the Cross of Calvary.

I renounce all fear of insanity, anguish, death wishes, suicide and death in the name of Jesus Christ. Death was conquered by Jesus Christ, and He alone holds the keys of death and hell, and I rejoice that He holds my life in His hands now. He came to give me life abundantly and eternally, and I believe His promises.

I renounce all anger, hatred, murderous thoughts, revenge, retaliation, spiritual apathy, false religion, all unbelief, especially unbelief in the Holy Bible as God's Word, and all compromise of God's Word. I renounce all spiritual searching into false religions, and all striving to please God. I rest in the knowledge that I have found my Lord and Saviour Jesus Christ, and that He has found me.

Holy Royal Arch Degree

In the name of Jesus Christ, I renounce and forsake the oaths taken and the curses involved in the Holy Royal Arch Degree especially the oath regarding the removal of the head from the body and the exposing of the brains to the hot sun. I renounce the false secret name of God, JAHBULON, and declare total rejection of all worship of the false pagan gods, BUL or Baal, and On or Osiris, I also renounce the password, AMMI RUHAMAH and all it means. I renounce the false communion or Eucharist taken in this degree, and all the mockery, skepticism and unbelief about the redemptive work of Jesus Christ on the cross of Calvary. I cut off all these curses and their effects on me and my family in the name of Jesus Christ, and I pray for... (healing of the brain, the mind etc.)

I renounce and forsake the oaths taken and the curses involved in the Royal Master Degree of the York Rite; the Select Master Degree with its penalty to have my hands chopped off to the stumps, to have my eyes plucked out from their sockets, and to have my body quartered and thrown among the rubbish of the Temple.

I renounce and forsake the oaths taken and the curses involved in the Super Excellent Master Degree along with the penalty of having my thumbs out off, my eyes put out, my body bound in fetters and brass, and conveyed captive to a strange land; and also of the Knights Order of the Red Cross, along with the penalty of having my house torn down and my being hanged on the exposed timbers.

I renounce the Knights Templar Degree and the secret words of KEB RAIOTH, and also Knights of Malta Degree and the secret words MAHER-SHALAL-HASH-BAZ.

I renounce the vows taken on a human skull, the crossed swords, and curse and death wish of Judas of having the head cut off and placed on top of a church spire. I renounce the unholy communion and especially of drinking from a human skull in many Rites.

18th Degree

I renounce the oaths taken and the curses and penalties involved in the Eighteenth Degree of Masonry, the Most Wise Sovereign Knight of the Pelican and the Eagle and Sovereign Prince Rose Croix of Heredom. I renounce and reject the Pelican witchcraft spirit, as well as the occultic influence of the Rosicrucians and the Kabbala in this degree.

I renounce the claim that the death of Jesus Christ was a "dire calamity," and also the deliberate mockery and twisting of the Christian doctrine of the Atonement. I renounce the blasphemy and rejection of the deity of Jesus Christ, and the secret words IGNE NATURA RENOVATUR INTEGRA and its burning, I renounce the mockery of the communion taken in this degree, including a biscuit, salt and white wine.

30th Degree

I renounce the oaths taken and the curses involved in the Thirtieth Degree of Masonry, the Grand Knight Kadosh and Knight of the Black and White Eagle. I renounce the secret passwords, STIBIUM ALKABAR, PHARASH-KOH and all they mean.

Sublime Princes of the Royal Secret (31st Degree)

I renounce the oaths taken and the curses involved in the Thirty-First Degree of Masonry, the Grand inspector Inquisitor Commander. I renounce all the gods and goddesses of Egypt which are honoured in this degree, including Anubis with the ram's head, Osiris the Sun god, Isis the sister and wife of Osiris and also the moon goddess. I renounce the Soul of Cheres, the false symbol of immortality, the Chamber of the dead and the false teaching of reincarnation.

32nd Degree

I renounce the oaths taken and the curses involved in the Thirty-Second Degree of Masonry, the Sublime Prince of the Royal Secret. I renounce the secret passwords, PHAAL/PHARASH-KOL and all they mean. I renounce Masonry's false trinitarian deity AUM, and its parts; Brahma the creator, Vishnu the preserver and Shiva the destroyer. I renounce the deity of AHURA-MAZDA, the claimed spirit or source of all light, and the worship with fire, which is an abomination to God, and also the drinking from a human skull in many Rites.

What is Freemasonry? 65

York Rite

I renounce and forsake the oaths taken and the curses involved in the York Rite Degrees of Masonry. I renounce the Mark Lodge, and the mark in the form of squares and angles which marks the person for life. I also reject the jewel or occult talisman which may have been made from this mark sign and worn at the lodge meetings; the Mark Master Degree with its secret word JOPPA, and its penalty of having the right ear smote off and the curse of permanent deafness, as well as the right hand being chopped off for being an imposter.

I also renounce and forsake the oaths taken and the curses involved in the other York Rite Degrees, including Past Master, with the penalty of having my tongue split from tip to root; and of the Most Excellent Master Degree, in which the penalty is to have my breast torn open and my heart and vital organs removed and exposed to rot on the dung hill.

Shriners

I renounce the oaths taken and the curses and penalties involved in the Ancient Arabic Order of the Nobles of the Mystic Shrine. I renounce the piercing of the eyeballs with a three edged blade, the flaying of the feet, the madness, and the worship of the false god Allah as the god of our fathers. I renounce the hoodwink, the mock hanging, the mock beheading, the mock drinking of the blood of the victim, the mock dog urinating on the initiate, and the offering of urine as a commemoration.

33rd & Supreme Degree

In the name of Jesus Christ I renounce the oaths taken and the curses involved in the supreme Thirty-Third Degree of Freemasonry, the Grand Sovereign

Inspector General. I renounce the secret passwords, DEMOLAY-HIRUM ABIFF, FREDERICK OF PRUSSIA, MICHA, MACHA, BEALIM, and ADONAI and all they mean. I renounce all the obligations of every Masonic degree, and all penalties invoked. I renounce and utterly forsake The Great Architect of The Universe, who is revealed in this degree as Lucifer, and his false claim to be the universal fatherhood of God. I renounce the cable-tow around the neck. I renounce the death wish that the wine drunk from human skull should turn to poison and the skeleton whose cold arms are invited if the oath of this degree is violated. I renounce the three infamous assassins of their grand master, law, property and religion and the greed and witchcraft involved in the attempt to manipulate and control the rest of mankind. In the name of God the Father, Jesus Christ the Son, and the Holy Spirit, I renounce and break the curses involved in the idolatry, blasphemy, secrecy and deception of Freemasonry at every level, and I appropriate the Blood of Jesus Christ to cleanse all the consequences of these from my life. I now revoke all previous consent given by any of my ancestors or myself to be deceived.

All other degrees

I renounce all other oaths taken, the rituals of every other degree and the curses involved. These include the Allied Degrees, The Red Cross of Constantine, the Order of the Secret Monitor, and the Masonic Royal Order of Scotland. I renounce all other lodges and secret societies including Prince Hall Freemasonry, Grand Orient Lodges, Mormonism, The Order of Amaranth, the Royal Order of Jesters, the Manchester Unity Order of Oddfellows, Buffalos, Druids, Foresters, the Orange and Black Lodges,

Elks, Moose and Eagles Lodges, the Ku Klux Klan, The Grange, the Woodmen of the World, Riders of the Red Robe, the Knights of Pythias, the Mystic Order of the Veiled Prophets of the Enchanted Realm, the women's Orders of the Eastern Star, of the Ladies Oriental Shrine, and of the White Shrine of Jerusalem, the girls' order of the Daughters of the Eastern Star, the International Orders of Job's Daughters, and of the Rainbow, and the boys' Order of De Molay, and their effects on me and all my family.

Lord Jesus, because you want me to be totally free from all occult bondages, I will burn all objects in my possession which connect me with all lodges and occultic organizations, including Masonry, Witchcraft and Mormonism, and all regalia, aprons, books of rituals, rings and other jewelry. I renounce the effects of these or other objects of Masonry, including the compass and the square, have had on me or my family, in the name of Jesus Christ.

I renounce every evil spirit associated with Masonry and Witchcraft and all other sins, and I command in the name of Jesus Christ for Satan and every evil spirit to be bound, and to leave me now, touching or harming no-one, and go to the place appointed for you by the Lord Jesus, never to return to me or my family. I call on the name of the Lord Jesus to be delivered of these spirits, in accordance with the many promises of the Bible. I ask to be delivered of every spirit of sickness, infirmity, curse, affliction, addiction, disease or allergy associated with these sins I have confessed and renounced. I surrender to God's Holy Spirit and to no other spirit all the places in my life where these sins have been.

(All participants should now be invited to sincerely carry out in faith the following actions):

(1) Symbolically remove the blindfold (hoodwink) and give it to the Lord for disposal;

(2) In the same way, symbolically remove the veil of mourning;

(3) Symbolically cut and remove the noose from around the neck, gather it up with the cable tow running down the body and give it to the Lord for His disposal;

(4) Renounce the false Freemasonry marriage covenant, removing from the 4th finger of the right hand the ring of this false marriage covenant, giving it to the Lord to dispose of it;

(5) Symbolically remove the chains and bondage of Freemasonry from your body;

(6) Symbolically remove all Freemasonry regalia and armor, especially the Apron;

(7) Invite participants to repent of and seek forgiveness for having walked on all unholy ground including Freemasonry lodges and temples, including any Mormon or any other occultic/Masonic organizations.

(8) Symbolically remove the ball and chain from the ankles.

(9) Proclaim that Satan and his demons no longer have any legal rights to mislead and manipulate the person seeking help.

Holy Spirit, I ask, that you show me anything else which I need to do or to pray so that I and my family may be totally free from the consequences of the sins of Masonry, Witchcraft, Mormonism and all related Paganism and Occultism.

(Pause, while listening to God, and pray as the Holy Spirit leads you.)

Now, dear Father God, I ask humbly for the blood of Jesus Christ, your Son and my Saviour, to cleanse me from all these sins I have confessed and renounced, to cleanse my spirit, my soul, my mind, my emotions and every part of my body which has been affected by these sins, in the name of Jesus Christ. I also command every cell in my body to come into divine order now, and to be healed and made whole as they were designed to be by my loving Creator, including restoring all chemical imbalances and neurological functions, controlling all cancerous cells, and reversing all degenerative diseases, in the name of the Lord Jesus Christ.

I surrender to God's Holy Spirit and to no other spirit all the places in my life where these sins have been.

"I ask you, Lord, to baptize me in your Holy Spirit now according to the promises in your Word. I take to myself the whole armor of God in accordance with Ephesians Chapter Six, and rejoice in its protection as Jesus surrounds me and fills me with His Holy Spirit. I enthrone you, Lord Jesus, in my heart, for you are my Lord and Saviour, the source of eternal life. Thank you, Father God, for your mercy, your forgiveness and your love, in the name of Jesus Christ, Amen."

Copying of this prayer is both permitted and encouraged provided reference is made to where it comes from. Written testimonies of changed lives and healings are welcome. Additions to this prayer will be added to our Internet site as well as for other lodges or secret or occultic organizations. These may be freely down-loaded for wider use. If additional prayer and ministry are required following the above prayer, please contact the Jubilee Essential Resources, who may refer you to someone closer to you. We have competent counselors in most countries around the world.

We also have a resignation letter that we found online that we give to people. We tell people to bind up the spirit of deception before giving it to someone. Also pray that as they read the resignation letter that they will have a revelation of the truth behind Freemasonry. We have had testimonies that many have given this resignation letter to family members, and they have actually gotten saved and come out of Freemasonry.

A Sample Resignation Letter

To the members of

(your lodge)

Greetings in the Name of Jesus Christ,

When I was initiated into Freemasonry, I was led to believe that my involvement would not interfere with my duty to God. Yet, I was led through three blood oaths in the three degrees of the Blue Lodge which are in direct violation of the commandment of Jesus Christ found in Matthew 5:33-37.

I have since come to realize that Freemasonry is a "Fraternal Order" which has a plan of salvation. The Masonic plan of salvation does not require faith in Jesus Christ, but rather depends on imitating Hiram Abiff. At many places, Masonic ritual encourages Masons to believe that they will go to heaven. Consider the Covering of a Lodge: it is "a clouded canopy or star-decked heaven where all good Masons hope at last to arrive." Consider the Three Steps "... as Master Masons, we may enjoy the happy reflections consequent on a well-spent life, and die in the hope of a glorious immortality." Consider the prayer just before Hiram is raised: "Yet, 0

Lord! have compassion on the children of Thy creation – and administer them comfort in the time of trouble, and save them with an everlasting salvation."

With all of this, Freemasonry is encouraging Master Masons to believe that they will go to heaven when they die. But just who are Master Masons? They include Hindus, Moslems, Buddhists and men of many other religions which reject the claims of Jesus. Freemasonry is encouraging false hope in unsaved men. Just after Hiram is raised, ritual tells us that we should imitate Hiram Abiff so that we can welcome death and get into heaven. The Bible is clear. John 14:6 contains the words of Jesus. He said "I am the way, the truth, and the life, no one comes to the father but by me."

It is obvious that Freemasonry is not following the teachings of Jesus, because ritual encourages lost souls that they will get into heaven. Ritual suggests imitation of Hiram Abiff as the way to the Celestial Lodge above. The book of 2 John verse 9 states: "Whosoever transgresseth, and abideth not in the doctrine of Christ, hath not God." When coupled with the fact that Masonic ritual teaches salvation on the basis of imitating Hiram Abiff, rather than Faith in Jesus Christ, it is clear from this verse that the Masonic Lodge does not have God. The GAOTU cannot be the God of the Bible, because it rejects the claims of His Son.

I know that many of you profess to be Christians. I would like to encourage each of you to examine and pray about the contents of Masonic ritual. As Christians, can we take part in an organization which teaches salvation without Jesus? Galatians 1:8-9 makes it clear that the penalty for teaching a false plan of salvation is condemnation. I encourage you to prayerfully consider these things.

The oaths which I took are null and void. God has released me from them. Leviticus 5:4-6 makes it clear that when something is hidden from a man and he takes an oath thoughtlessly, he is guilty of sin. When he recognizes it as sin, he may be released from it by confessing it as sin, and claiming the promise found in first John 1:8-9.

I want you to know that I am not rejecting you, as individuals; however, I am totally rejecting Freemasonry. I want nothing more to do with it, now, or at any time in the future. I do not want a demit, which allows joining another Lodge. I am no longer a Mason.

I encourage each of you to get out of the Lodge. I pray that my involvement in Freemasonry will not result in the loss of anyone's soul, because he believed the promises and the rituals. The Masonic plan of salvation is a ticket to hell. I encourage each of you to read the book of John in your Masonic Bible. Read it again and again until you know the truth.

Blessings in Jesus,
(Your signature)

Chapter 7

Deliverance Brings Healing

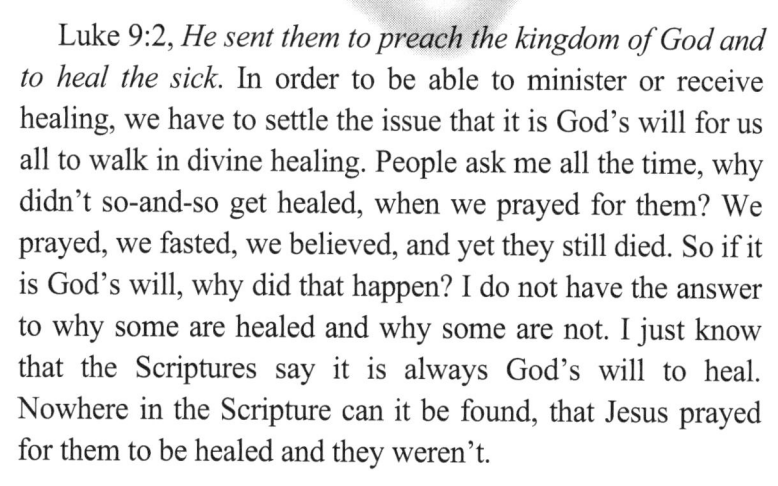

Luke 9:2, *He sent them to preach the kingdom of God and to heal the sick.* In order to be able to minister or receive healing, we have to settle the issue that it is God's will for us all to walk in divine healing. People ask me all the time, why didn't so-and-so get healed, when we prayed for them? We prayed, we fasted, we believed, and yet they still died. So if it is God's will, why did that happen? I do not have the answer to why some are healed and why some are not. I just know that the Scriptures say it is always God's will to heal. Nowhere in the Scripture can it be found, that Jesus prayed for them to be healed and they weren't.

Could it be the person praying was not praying in faith? James 5:15, *"And the prayer of faith will save the sick, and the Lord will raise him up. And if he has committed sins, he will be forgiven."* Or the person being prayed for had an open door for the enemy to have legal right to afflict them? Maybe they had doubt and unbelief regarding their healing. As I said, I don't have the answer to why some are healed, and others not, but it does not change the Word of God. Mark 16:18 says, *"They will take up serpents; and if they drink anything deadly, it will by no means hurt them; they will lay hands on the sick, and they will recover."* Is this the Word of God? Then it is true. Circumstances and experiences do not change what the Word says.

I do know that we have prayed for people who had cancer, and they were healed. There was a man in a church who had cancer of the esophagus. We prayed for him and when he went for his PET and CAT scans, he was 100 percent cancer free. We have seen many healed of cancer when we have prayed for them. The way we minister healing to someone is to cast out the spirit of death or infirmity, sometimes both. Deliverance and healing go hand-in-hand. We first cast out the demon of infirmity and then we impart the healing. As we talked about in an earlier chapter, sometimes we inherit sickness and disease from our ancestors. So we may have to break it off generationally too. As was the case of the man we ministered to from Minnesota. We received a call from this man and his wife. He had been diagnosed with cancer and had heard of us and wanted to come for ministry. As we began to pray for him, the Lord showed us that in his family line was Freemasonry, and the Freemasonry had opened him up for a spirit of premature death and cancer. So we ministered deliverance and healing and received an awesome testimony from him a few months later. He said that his PSA level was back down to being undetectable. He was healed. We rejoiced with him and his wife. They have now joined a local healing team where they are from, and when they come to Florida on vacation, they join our healing and deliverance team. They are able to minister with not only compassion, but with authority because of what they have seen God do in the area of healing.

Many of us have an Old Testament mindset that says we have to do something to get our healing, or to even be used to bring forth healing. Most people are waiting on a prophetic word to tell them that they have a healing anointing or that God wants to use them to heal others. We already have the written word, and the Lord said in Luke 10:9 *"and heal the sick there, and say to them the kingdom of God has come near to you."*

I have heard people say that the Lord put sickness on them to keep them holy, and to teach them something. Dr. Bill Hamon references A.B. Simpson, as the one who had the first restorative truth about divine healing, in his book *The Eternal Church*. Simpson said, "If the blood of Jesus and the grace of God, and the power of the Holy Spirit are not sufficient to keep you humble and holy. I do not see how sickness is going to unless sickness is a greater Savior than Christ."

Dr. Simpson also said, "If sickness is God teaching someone something through their sickness, then every doctor and hospital are moving in rebellion instead of mercy if sickness is God's will."

So instead of waiting on a specific word to minister healing, know that it will come as we minister in faith, according to His Word. It is like the Lord wrote a personal letter to you. Saying son or daughter, I want to heal you and use you to heal others. But a spirit of religion, those things that we have been taught in churches growing up would say; you must do it this way. That you must cross the T's and dot the I's, follow a formula. If God had a formula, he would have put it in His Word, so that we could follow it. The enemy will come at your mind and say, "Do you really think God could use you to heal the sick?" God doesn't have you go pray for someone and then sits back to see if you can do it. He is with you, El Shaddai. *When Abram was ninety-nine years old, the Lord appeared to Abram and said to him, "I am Almighty God; walk before me and be blameless"* (Gen. 17:1). Everywhere we go, Jesus is with us. When people say they are following Christ, it sounds like they are running to catch up with Him. It's the desire of the Lord to heal people. By His stripes we are healed, not by His stripes we *hope* we will be healed.

What is the greatest hindrance to healing? It is doubt, unbelief and fear. Doubt and unbelief says I don't know that God can heal this person. Fear says what if I pray for them and they don't get healed? What will people think?

The word salvation in Greek is, Soteria. It implies deliverance, preservation, healing, health and soundness. The Greek word Sozo, translated saved also means healed, made whole. Romans 10:9 says *that if you confess with your mouth the Lord Jesus and believe in your heart, that God has raised him from the dead, you will be saved.*

Both Greek words for salvation and saved mean, both physical and spiritual salvation. Or we can say spiritual and physical healing. *"For the husband is head of the wife, as also Christ is head of the church, and He is the savior of the body"* (Eph. 5:23).

I have read several books on healing. I looked at several great healing ministers including John G. Lake, FF Bosworth, A.B. Simpson, Smith Wigglesworth, Aimee Simple McPherson, and TL Osborn to try and see what made their ministries so successful in the area of healing. One thing they had in common was just plain faith. They believed

God's Word. It wasn't even that they were so special; it was because they got it, they really got it. They understood the simplicity of the Gospel. Jesus said do it and they did. They read the Word of God and believed it. It wasn't that they had angelic visitation where a healing anointing was imparted. It wasn't anything supernatural, but just simply that they had a revelation as they read the Scriptures on healing that it is for now, and that we can pray for the sick and see them healed. They didn't let circumstances move them.

They all agreed that healing is our covenant with God and that we need to have faith to believe for it. It doesn't mean that the person being prayed for necessarily had to have faith to be healed, but the one doing the praying needs to believe it is true. The person that is healed needs to become active in keeping the healing. Most healing ministers when they pray for someone, say for example, someone who has a hard time walking; they have them stand up and walk. People who have back problems, they have them bend over and touch the floor. They have them do an action of faith.

Also we need to confess our healing and not doubt it, especially if there is not an immediate manifestation of the healing. After Hezekiah was healed it took three days before he was strong enough to go to the house of the Lord. Second Kings 20:1-5, *"In those days Hezekiah was sick and near death. And Isaiah the prophet, the son of Amoz, went to him and said to him, "Thus says the Lord: 'set your house in order, for you shall die, and not live.'" ²Then he turned his face toward the wall, and prayed to the Lord, saying, ³ 'Remember now, O lord, I pray, how I have walked before You in truth, and with a loyal heart, and have done what was good in your site.' And Hezekiah wept bitterly. ⁴And it happened, before Isaiah had gone out into the middle court, that the word of the Lord came to him, saying, ⁵'Return and tell Hezekiah, the leader of My people, "Thus says the Lord, the God of David your father: "I have heard your prayer, I have seen your tears, surely I will heal you. On the third day you shall go up to the house of the Lord."*

A miracle is instant, healing is not. So we need to understand the difference between a miracle and healing.

All the famous healing ministers agreed that healing is in the atonement. The corresponding New Testament words are hilamos and propitiation. 1 John 2:2; 1 John 4:10; Romans 3:25 and Hebrews 9:5 refers to the Mercy seat and describes the means, the person and the work of the Lord Jesus Christ in His death on the cross. The shedding of His blood is his vicarious sacrifice for sin, by which God shows mercy to sinners.[5]

Deliverance from sickness is provided for in the atonement. It is the privilege of all believers based on Isaiah 53:4-5. *"Surely he has borne our griefs And carried our sorrows; yet we esteemed Him stricken, Smitten by God, and afflicted. ⁵But He was wounded for our transgressions, He was bruised for our iniquities; the chastisement for our peace was upon Him, and by His stripes we are healed."*

It is important for us to teach that healing is for us as Christians. FF Bosworth, in his book *Christ the Healer* says "the first step to being healed is the same as the first step toward salvation, or any other blessing that God promises. This person needs to know what the Bible teaches about healing." Leviticus 14:18, *"The rest of the oil that is in the priest's hand he shall put on the head of him who is to be*

---
[5] From Vine's Expository Dictionary of Biblical words, copyright (c) 1985, Thomson Nelson.

cleansed. So the priest shall make atonement for him before the Lord." Why was there atonement for the leper's healing if healing for us is not in the atonement of Christ?

FF Bosworth also says that hundreds of people were healed just by listening to his preaching on the subject of healing in the atonement. No one laid hands on them and prayed for them. They were healed through their own faith, while listening to the Word about healing.

I'm really happy that we don't have to be like the dying Israelites who had to look at a serpent on a pole for their healing. Personally, I hate snakes. Numbers 21:8-9, *"Then the Lord said to Moses, 'make a fiery serpent, and set it on a pole; and it shall be that everyone who is bitten, when he looks at it, shall live.' ⁹So Moses made a bronze serpent, and put it on a pole; and so it was, if a serpent had bitten anyone, when he looked at the bronze serpent, he lived."*

A serpent on the pole represented looking to Jesus our healer. Looking to what he purchased for us on Calvary. The last Adam was sent to take away all the first Adam brought upon us. We know in the Garden of Eden, there was no sickness until sin entered in.

Healing is part of our covenant with God. The word covenant means an agreement between two people or two groups that involves promises on the part of each to the other. The concept of covenant between God and His people is one of the most important theological truths of the Bible. Remember Abraham, God had a covenant with Abraham, God promised to bless Abraham's descendents and to make them His special people. A covenant in the biblical sense implies much more than a contract or simple agreement. If we sign a business contract, there is always a date of when it begins and when it ends. There is no ending to our covenant with God. No hidden motives in the covenant.

He said, "If you listen carefully to the voice of the Lord your God and do what is right in His eyes, if you pay attention to His commands and keep all His decrees, I will not bring on you any of the diseases I brought on the Egyptians, for I am the Lord, who heals you" (Exod. 15:26 New International Version).

It is both the Old and New Testament revelation. But some of the famous healing ministers did move in the supernatural, because they realized that God is a supernatural God. As His children we too can see the supernatural happen when we pray. The word supernatural in Webster's Dictionary is defined as existing or occurring through some agency beyond the known forces of nature. Believed to be miraculous or divine, super means above, and natural means nature. So it is above nature. Jesus wants to release miracles through us as believers. Psalms 103:2-4 says, *"bless the Lord, O my soul, and forget not all His benefits: ³Who forgives all your iniquities, who heals all your diseases, ⁴Who redeems your life from destruction."*

One of the names of the Lord is Jehovah Rapha, it is translated "I am the Lord, thy physician or I am the Lord that Healeth thee." It doesn't say He's the Lord that leaves you sick.

Dr. Hamon, our overseer says which is easier for God to do? Save you or heal you? *So He got into a boat, crossed over, and came to His own city. ²Then behold, they brought to Him, a paralytic lying on a bed. When Jesus saw their faith, He said to the paralytic, "Son be of good cheer; your sins are forgiven you." ³And at once, some of the scribes said within themselves, "This man blasphemes!" ⁴But Jesus, knowing their thoughts, said, "Why do you think evil in your hearts? ⁵For which is easier to say, "Your sins are forgiven you," or to say, "Arise and walk." ⁶But that you may know that the Son of Man has power on earth to forgive sins." Then he said to paralytic, "Arise, take up your bed, and go to your house." ⁷And he arose and departed to his house. ⁸Now when the multitudes saw it, they marveled and glorified God, who had given such power to men* (Matt. 9:1-8).

Jesus treated sin and sickness the same, He removed them. Dr. Hamon also says if you can't do it for your sake, then do it for Jesus. Jesus took those stripes for our healing and if we don't believe, then Jesus suffered in vain. Have you seen the movie *The Passion of the Christ* with Mel Gibson? The part where He is being beaten with the cat of nine tails is horrible. His flesh is being ripped off of His body. Do you know that beating was for our healing? Don't let Him have suffered in vain.

So if Jesus already did it, there is nothing we have to do to get our healing. Praying and fasting won't make you a miracle worker. It is only by believing what is said in the Word about healing. Also people being healed or being delivered needs to become as simple as getting them saved. The Lord wants us to get to that place where there is no sick among us. It's time to see cancer, and every other disease, bow its knee to the Name of Jesus. The believer, the saints of God, should be going around doing what it says in Matthew 10:1. *"And when He had called His twelve disciples to Him, He gave them power over unclean spirits, to cast them out, and to heal all kinds of sickness and all kinds of disease."* Did it say except cancer? Did it say except diabetes? Did it say all? What does all mean? It means all, everything.

This is part of the Apostolic commission to the church and to us as individuals. Matthew 9:35, *"Then Jesus went about all the cities and villages, teaching in their synagogues, preaching the gospel of the kingdom, and healing every sickness in every disease among the people.* Matthew 10:1, *and when he called his twelve disciples to Him, He gave them power over unclean spirits, to cast them out, and to heal all kinds of sickness and all kinds of diseases.* Matthew 10:7-8, *"And as you go, preach, saying, "the kingdom of heaven is at hand." ⁸"Heal the sick, cleanse the lepers, raise the dead," cast out demons.*

Matthew 10:8, "Freely you have received, freely give." Jesus commissioned not only His disciples, but He commissioned us to do the same as He did. This is talking about us taking dominion. God is calling each one of us to be the ones that will go into the world and change it. Make it look like Jesus.

I personally have been healed of many things. In 1995, I contracted the herpes virus and I lost my eyesight. I must have touched something that had a live virus on it and then touched my eyes. I woke up one morning with terrible pain in my eyes. It felt like somebody was sticking needles in my eyes. I also noticed my eyes were really red and my vision was getting blurry. The next day most of my eyesight was gone. So I made an appointment with a doctor. A friend of mine drove me there. This was on a Saturday so it wasn't his normal office hours. He had his two children with him. When he looked at my eyes, he asked my friend Marie to take his children outside. He sat me in the chair and looked at my eyes through a machine. I guess he already suspected that I had herpes and that is why he had Marie take his children outside. He told me that that I had contracted the virus, and it was in my left eye, which is the one where the eyesight was almost gone. It was also in my right eye. He said what probably happened was that I had touched a shopping cart, a water faucet, something that someone else who had the virus touched. And it was still alive, and when I touched it with my hands I must've also touched my eyes. He went on to say that there is no cure and that the prognosis was permanent blindness. The only thing that he could do for me was to give me some Novocain drops, to help with the pain.

I remember the first thought that went through my mind was that I was a widow raising my sons. How would I be able to function as a blind person? I told my friend Marie what the doctor had said as we got into the car to drive home. She began to pray in tongues. We stopped to get my prescription of the Novocain drops and then proceeded to go home. At that time I was working for Christian International Ministries in the seminar department. Also, I was in the middle of building a new home. I was not able to be in the sunlight without terrible pain. So when I got home I went up to my bedroom and closed the curtains. Not realizing this was the plan of the enemy to keep me isolated. This is how the enemy works, he tries to get you to isolate and withdraw. Then he works overtime in your thoughts, in your mind.

He began to tell me that this was my future that I needed to accept what the doctor had said; that there was no cure. And that I would be blind for the rest of my life. I remember thinking of the movie of Helen Keller that I had watched years ago, and what it would be like to be a blind person. So for almost two weeks, I pretty much stayed up in my bedroom in the dark.

There was a wonderful lady from our church, who was like a spiritual mom to me. Her name was Beverly Donner, but we all called her Miss B. Well, Miss B. offered to come over to our house and cook for me and my sons. I was also packing to move into our new home. So she offered to help with that too. I remember she was down in the living room, packing my glassware. I was upstairs in my bedroom, but had the door open. Miss. B. would say, "Honey, all things work together for good to those that love God and are called according to His purpose." I remember thinking; I wish I could be more like her. As long as I had known her she never spoke doubt out of her mouth. She only spoke faith in what the Word said. But I think there was also a part of me that felt sorry for myself. Here I was a widow raising my sons, and now I am going blind. Doesn't the Word say that "God gives a blessing, and He adds no sorrow to it." My new house was a blessing, but yet I was going through sorrow. I would like to tell you that I stood in faith. But the truth is; I began believing the lie of the enemy. As Miss B. began to speak Scriptures and faith I noticed my spirit began to agree with the words she was speaking.

The next morning I got ready to go to work. I remember driving and not being able to see so well. I probably should have gotten someone to drive me, but I knew that I couldn't stay in that bedroom any longer listening to the lies of the enemy. I needed to be back at work, and with people who could encourage me.

I went to church on Sunday, and there was a mighty move of the Spirit that day. Our pastor had just come back from Jamaica. The Holy Spirit touched him while he was preaching, and he was slain in the Spirit on the stage. There was such a strong anointing of the presence of God. A lady in our church, who had moved from Benny Hinn's ministry came up to me and said, "I have been waiting for this anointing to pray for your eyes." I have since learned that we don't have to wait for the anointing that we carry the anointing. She laid hands on me and imparted healing. She told me that by 11 o'clock that night I would have my eyesight back. She said, "It will be like layers coming off of your eyes." And it happened just like she said.

I went back to the doctor to share with him what had happened and have him examine my eyes again. Even though I could see, and my eyes had cleared up, he was still skeptical. He said I still had herpes, because remember the medical field says there is no cure. He said to me that if I ever became stressed out or got sick that it would come back. I walked out of his office and immediately said, in the Name of Jesus, I break off every word curse that was just spoken over me and every diagnosis from him and I thank you Lord that I am healed. That was years ago. I have walked through a lot of stress, and some sicknesses. But my eyes are healed.

I remember a few years ago, when I was ministering in Nova Scotia, Canada, my eyes became blurry. Immediately, the thought came to my mind, oh no it's trying to come back. So I made an appointment with an eye doctor in Canada. As my husband and I were sitting in the waiting room, I asked my husband if I should share with the doctor about the herpes virus and losing my sight. My husband said to me,

"Why would you want to tell them about losing your sight. Weren't you healed?" That was the key for me. God doesn't do anything halfway. And if He healed me then I'm healed. It showed me that the enemy will come around again, knocking on the door trying to get you to accept that you are not healed. We have to be wise and understand his tactics and how he works. So I repented and broke agreement with the enemy. The doctor examined me and said my eyes were in good shape and my peripheral vision was great.

That isn't the only healing that I had in my life. I had many sicknesses when I was little. I was also epileptic, and God healed me of that. Then in 2002 I had a sore on the calf of my left leg. It didn't seem to want to heal. Whenever I bumped it or touched it, there was an awful burning pain. So after a few months of it not going away I made an appointment with a dermatologist. He took a biopsy of it. The next week I got a call from his office and they said it was cancerous. I remember the shock of the call. I hung up the phone and told my husband. The nurse said that they would be making an appointment for me to see a plastic surgeon. I found out that most skin cancer surgery is done by a plastic surgeon. We prayed about it with our pastors, and we felt to have the surgery.

> We always tell people that we are not against doctors or taking medicine, but that it should only be a temporary thing. Taking medicine can open you up to a spirit of Pharmakia. The word for medicine or pharmacy is pharmakia:
>
> SORCERY 1. pharmakia (or—eia) NT:5331 (Eng., "pharmacy," etc.) primarily signified "the use of medicine, drugs, spells"; "poisoning"; "sorcery," Galations 5:20, RV, "sorcery" (KJV, "witchcraft"),

mentioned as one of "the works of the flesh." (See also Rev. 9:21; 18:23; Exod. 7:11, 22; 8:7, 18; Isa. 47:9, 12) In "sorcery," the use of drugs, whether simple or potent, was generally accompanied by incantations and appeals to occult powers, with the provision of various charms, amulets, etc., professedly designed to keep the applicant or patient from the attention and power of demons, but actually to impress the applicant with the mysterious resources and powers of the sorcerer.

2. MAGIA (or—eia) NT: 3095, "the magic art," is used in the plural in Acts 8:11, sorceries (see SORCERER, No. 1). mageuo NT:3096, akin to A, No. 2, "to practice magic," Acts 8:9, "used sorcery," is used as in A, No. 2, of Simon Magnus.[6]

One of the definitions of pharmakia is poison. Have you ever seen some of the commercials for medicines? It starts off advertising a particular medicine for a particular problem and then at the end of the commercial, it says there may be some side effects. It goes like this. "Take this medicine for your high blood pressure or your back pain. But the side effects can be kidney failure, heart attack or even loss of life." So although we are not against medicine, we do believe healing is a better way to go.

I ended up having the surgery, and the doctor cut out the cancer. He was able to get it all. We believe that the Lord used the doctor in this situation to remove the cancer. I was released from the hospital that same day, and we also believe because of prayer that I didn't have to take any pain medication. I chose to not have reconstructive surgery on my leg, and it healed just fine without it. I only have a very small scar there.

---

[6] From Vine's Expository Dictionary of Biblical Words, Copyright © 1985, Thomas Nelson Publishers.

The next year in 2003 I began to have some pain in my abdomen. I actually began to gain weight and my stomach was protruding some. I went to a doctor and she examined me and sent me for an ultrasound. The ultrasound showed that I had numerous tumors. The doctor said she would need to do a hysterectomy. Because I had my three sons by caesarian section I would not be able to have the surgery without being cut open. So in order to have this drastic of a surgery I had to go through a lot of tests. I had to have heart tests, urinalysis, blood work, and a mammogram.

One of the tests I had came back and it looked like I had uterine cancer. I had gone out of town and was not returning until the Sunday before the surgery. When I got home I had several messages from my doctor's office asking me to call them. They had me come in right away. What I found out was that my doctor needed to do a biopsy to rule out uterine cancer. The tests came back in three days, and I was fine. She also said at that time the mammogram showed something. But she said the tests are not always accurate. So, just like the tests were wrong about the uterine cancer, they could be wrong about the mass in the breast.

She said she was going to go ahead with the surgery to remove the tumors. She would not know until she biopsied the tumors whether they were malignant or benign. So I had the surgery, and they removed all the tumors. This was major stomach surgery, and yet I was released from the hospital in two days. Once again, there was a quick healing, and I didn't have to take pain medication after leaving the hospital. Also, the tumors were all benign.

I went to get the staples removed from my stomach the next week. The doctor said she wanted me to have a sonogram of my breast. So it was scheduled for the end of the week. I received a phone call from my doctor saying that the sonogram showed a mass in my left breast. She said she was turning me over to a different surgeon. So we met with the surgeon and the operation was scheduled for the next week. Two days to the day I was lying on the operating table again. It was a very stressful time. The enemy was bombarding my mind with thoughts of death. My husband told me that God was going to heal me. And that the devil could not kill me. We had churches and friends all over the world praying for me. Our pastors anointed me with oil and prayed and agreed also. We have a ministers training college here at Christian International and all the students were also praying for me.

So after the surgery I was scheduled for a follow-up appointment. The surgeon said that when he went in to remove the mass, there was nothing there. We asked him if he removed it, if not, where did the mass that the ultrasound showed go? He kind of mumbled. Actually, he mumbled a lot. My husband and I looked at each other and wondered why he was mumbling and confused? The bottom line was that he had no explanation of what happened to the mass. He informed me that he put in a titanium locator. That way, whenever I get a mammogram they can go back to where the mass was. Keyword is "was." I was a little upset about having this locator in me, but the Lord said it was okay, because it's a documented miracle. This is just one more time I received a healing miracle in my body.

A few years later, my father-in-law was in his late eighties and struggling with congestive heart failure. His ankles and legs were extremely swollen. They had him on massive doses of water pills. He was so swollen that he actually had to lift his legs up at times with his hands. We got a phone call on a Saturday morning from his heart doctor's office. They said that the blood work that he had had earlier in the week showed that he was in renal failure. They said for us to take him to the emergency room. He would probably have to be on dialysis.

My father and mother-in-law lived in a two-bedroom house attached to ours. So my husband went over to their house and told my father-in-law that we needed to take him to the hospital. My father-in-law said he wanted to finish breakfast and then he would get ready. I jumped in the shower and got dressed. As I was blow drying my hair I said to the Lord, this is not right. We pray for people with cancer, broken bones, and back problems. All sorts of diseases, and Lord, you heal them. And now my father-in-law's kidneys are failing. He might have to go on dialysis?

I went to the living room and got my anointing oil, and went next door. I asked my father-in-law if I could anoint him and pray for him. He said yes.

When we got to the emergency room at Sacred Heart they began to run tests, they did urinalysis and blood work. He had three doctors who came in and examined him. The one doctor pressed on his kidneys and said, "Doesn't that hurt? Well if you are in renal failure it should hurt when I press on your kidneys."

He was at the hospital till late at night going through test after test. But they could find no renal failure. They released him to go home. My husband said as they were going by the nurses' station that they couldn't believe they were releasing him. All they did was give him instructions to see the cardiologist on Tuesday.

On Sunday morning, my husband came back from his parent's house and told me I had to go over and look at his dad's legs. My first thought was that there was more swelling. I went over and saw that his legs and ankles were no longer swollen. I asked him if he spent a lot of time in the bathroom last night. He said he hadn't and that when he woke up the swelling was just gone. We had another miracle. On Tuesday when he went to his heart doctor, the doctor just shook his head and said that this went against all his medical books and training, and that he wished he could take credit for it. But that he didn't do it and he pointed his finger toward heaven and said he did it, referring to the Lord, and that it was a miracle. When my father-in-law died, he was not in renal failure; his heart began to slow down and it just quit. No heart attack, no disease ravishing his body. His heart just stopped and he went to be with the Lord.

This is the way it should be for all of us. That we close our eyes, and we are in the presence of the Lord. No suffering, no pain. I know many of us have lost our loved ones to disease. But that does not change the Word of God. My hope is that by sharing some of my testimony regarding healing that it will bring a revelation, and a passion within you to pray for the sick. For you to know and believe that God still does heal. The old cliché is that God is still in the healing business. He really is.

Chapter 8
The Healing Centre – Beulah Restoration Centre

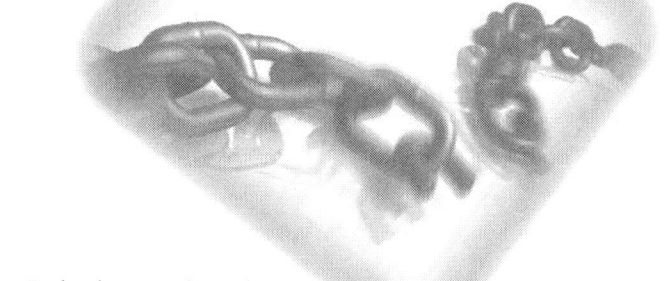

I had mentioned A.B. Simpson, who had the first restorative truth about divine healing. He was born in Prince Edward Island, Canada, December, 1843. To quote A.W. Tozer, from his book *Wingspread* that he wrote on Simpson's life, he said, "The world's greatest men usually enter the world incognito." This was true of Albert Benjamin Simpson. He was called to the ministry at the age of seventeen. He graduated from Knox College in Toronto, Canada. He was a Presbyterian minister with an anointing for evangelism. Years later he moved to New York City. He soon out grew the denomination he was in and founded Christian Missionary and Alliance. He also founded the first Bible College in the United States Nyack – Bible College in Nyack, New York.

In his early thirties, he began to have heart trouble. It was so severe that he had to give up all his pastoral duties and ministry. A prominent physician told him his days were numbered. It was during this time he searched the Scriptures and the Holy Spirit illuminated his mind with the reality that Jesus had a provision for the divine healing of our bodily ailments, just as he had for the forgiveness of our sins.

Simpson received a healing miracle of a brand new heart. He did more in his last days of ministry than the first years. He was an author and wrote over seventy books, and forty Hymns. He also was the author of a weekly magazine.[7]

In 2002 we told Dr. Hamon that we had bought property in Prince Edward Island, Canada. And we had found out that A.B. Simpson was born there. He told us to re-dig the wells of healing. Our property at that time was on the east end of the island. We knew Simpson was from somewhere on the North Shore. At that time we had not met any of Simpson's family. In 2005 we were out for a drive on the North Shore, and we saw a real estate sign on a corner lot. My husband felt called to take down the number and call the realtor. We got out and walked on the land. The land bordered Cavendish Road, and Simpson Mill Road. We had no idea when we saw the Simpson Mill sign that it meant A.B. Simpson's family. So we made an offer on the property and after a few counter offers they accepted our price. As we were in the realtor's office the Lord spoke to me that we had just bought Simpson land. I began to cry. I am sure the realtor wondered what was going on. He probably was thinking, boy she must really like this property! He had no idea that we had just walked into our destiny of starting a Healing Centre.

The next thing we had to do was sell our property on the east end of the island. So we put it up for sale with the realtor, but it took three years to sell. It was a beautiful two bedroom house with an acre of land on the water. We couldn't understand why it took so long to sell it. We even began to question were we to build the Centre. I remember what my pastor told me. She said, "What God says in the light

---
[7] Taken from Dr. Bill Hamon's book *The Eternal Church*.

He doesn't change His mind in the dark." So we stood and declared that our house would sell. That was in the spring of 2008. I was ministering in England that July, and I had a dream two nights in a row that our house in Canada sold. I even called my husband and told him that. Two weeks later he called me in England, to tell me that we had an offer on the house. We accepted the offer and had a closing date of August 5, 2008. So I flew home from England, and then we flew to Canada to begin to pack up our house for the move.

We began to look at plans to build a healing center. The healing center was to be twofold. It was to be a place for ministers to come to receive personal healing and freedom, but it was also to be a Centre to train others in the area of healing and deliverance. We met with the contractor and signed the papers. It was perfect. The Lord gave us a launch date of June 27, 2009. They started building, and it was to be finished the first week of December.

We were blessed that Dr. Hamon was ministering on the island that August. He and his wife Evelyn prayed over the property, and they both felt that God was going to use it mightily for training and healing.

The Lord gave us the name Beulah Restoration Centre. This goes along with our ministry name of Isaiah 62:4. We had just returned once again from England the end of November, and then flew back to Canada the beginning of December to close on the building of the center. My husband had planned on coming back in February to finish out the walls in the rooms of the center.

Our oldest son, Del became very ill the beginning of February. He had been diagnosed with MRSA. He had two operations at one hospital and a third one at Sacred Heart Hospital in Pensacola, Florida. He was very critical and not expected to live. It was not an easy situation to see your son lying in a hospital bed with a hole in the middle of his chest. He also had a hole in his right side that exposed his organs. I knew in my heart that God could and would heal him. I would stand by his bed and pray. I would make a declaration that he would live and not die. It would turn out to be several months before he walked in his healing. We cannot even imagine the pain that he went through. There were times when I would have to leave the room and just cry, because of all the suffering he was going through. But I never lost hope, or trust in the Lord. We had to battle almost every day for his life. I thank the Lord that I am in a church and ministry that has a powerful intercessory team. Christy is the name of the lady that oversees and leads the team. We spoke, almost daily, sometimes three and four times a day about what the doctors were saying. She would relay the message to the teams and they would agree in prayer for this specific situation. We know that the effectual fervent prayer of the righteous availeth much. Also, another man from the Ministry, Billy, started a prayer support group for our son Del on Facebook. It was so awesome seeing the body of Christ rally around us and our son. That April, Del had reconstructive surgery to close the wounds. They grafted skin from his legs and he spent another week in the hospital recovering. When they released him they put him in a big brace so that he would not rub his grafts because if he rubbed them they could move out of place. It takes some time for the grafts to take. Though the battle was intense the Lord did it again. It was a miracle that our son lived.

So, we are into April, and the center is supposed to be launched June 27. We were not able to go to Canada, because we spent two months at the hospital with Del. But God has blessed us with awesome people in our lives. Our pastor friends from Halifax, Nova Scotia, Earl and Lynn, went over almost every weekend and worked on the center to complete it. There was another church in Nova Scotia that brought a team over to put up all the drywall. So we were able to launch the center on June 27, 2009. We had several training conferences there already, and we saw many healings happen there. We are expecting it to be a place where the miraculous flows continuously. We will have training conferences twice a month at the Beulah location and travel the other two weekends to train, teach and minister.

We are dual based in Santa Rosa Beach, Florida, and Prince Edward Island, Canada. I thank the Lord that He has placed us in two of the most beautiful places in the world. And also that we have the privilege of seeing his healing power manifested in people's lives. There is no on-site lodging at the center. But where the center is located in the village of Cavendish, it is a major tourist area. You may have heard of *Anne of Green Gables* by the famous author, Lucy Maud Montgomery. The center is one mile down the road from Green Gables. So there are lots of bed and breakfasts, lodges and hotels within a mile where people can stay. We encourage people that when they come for the training for ministry to have some time to enjoy the island. Prince Edward Island is one of the largest exporters of lobster and mussels in the world.

This is a prophetic word given by Dr. Bill and Evelyn Hamon over the Centre.

Dr. Bill Hamon - Prince Edward Island

Father God we thank you that we have an inheritance in you. And you said the righteous should inherit the land. And Lord we thank you for this land that you have provided for your servants, your son and daughter. We decree right now Lord that people will be saved, filled, healed and Lord that many things will be for the Kingdom of God upon this Land.

Lord we just bring divine contacts with key leaders in this area and people that will come over and be a part of what is going on here Lord.

And that this will be a launching pad for them and their ministry and a place of joy and relaxation and fulfillment Lord. Even the children can come up and relax and enjoy being here. And Lord there would be a wonderful blessing upon it.

And we just release right now God Prophetically that this is going to be a lighthouse for you and Lord I just see people coming in and being talked to, ministered to and then they are coming in Clandestine and a secret because they are well known people and they are from old order churches and they are from situations and they don't want other people to know they went to a public meeting. So they will come here and receive healing, prophecy and ministry, you will bring transformation and healing to them.

And Lord we release the blessings of God upon this property. It is dedicated to the Lord, it's sanctified of God, and it's dedicated to the Glory of God for the Kingdom of God's purposes.

We agree and decree and so it be. In Jesus' Name

Mom Hamon

I feel it's really blessed and I feel the anointing of God out here. I just feel the presence of the Lord, it's just a wonderful, wonderful place. I believe it's going to bring peace to many people and deliverance and just feel God is in this. I am thankful to be here.

Dr. Hamon also gave us this word personally.

Bishop Bill Hamon – Prince Edward Island, Canada

Father we bless the man and woman of God right now and we release your grace and power upon them. Lord you called them to be an Apostle and Prophet Team to co-labor together to bring deliverance at Zion. And God to be delivers in Zion as you said you would raise up deliverers in Zion. And you would raise up those who would bring restoration, restoration. As Isaiah said "non sayeth restore" but Joel says "God will Restore."

And the Lord says I made you deliverers and restorers, deliverers and restorers. You will deliver and then restore. Deliver and restore. The Lord says get ready now you're moving to another phase of your ministry. You're moving to another expansion. And the Lord says you will go to Nation after Nation. But then I am going to have you have a way to those different nations. They will say don't come and go here, here and there but come and teach and train for three weeks. Come and teach and train until we can reproduce.

And I release that reproducing training, equipping, activating anointing within you now. And the Lord says you will no longer go to the many places but you will go to one place and they will all gather together at that one place. So you can teach, train and equip and reproduce that they may go forth. And the Lord says you will multiply yourselves many times over. And I will break the bonds of the enemy of fear and doubt and every affliction that the enemy had come against you with.

I rebuke him Now sayeth the Lord.

Because you called them with the anointing to set the captives free and open the prison doors and bring the Spirit of anointing of God upon my people. The Lord says son and daughter get ready, get ready, I am finishing the work I began in you and I am moving you to a new level to a new dimension. And you will headquarter here and headquarter there and headquarter over there. And the Lord says you will have different places you will stay and go and do.

And the Lord says you will be mother and father, you will be like sitting hens and sitting on eggs that will hatch many and you will have many chicks that will come forth and you will bring forth many that will become those that will become meat on the table, those that will become reproducers, that will lay more eggs and bring forth more ministry, more anointing and raise up others.

The Lord says I will give you that reproducing anointing now to reproduce, reproduce, reproduce. And you will train and equip. I will give you the time, the place, the energy and resources and the people. Lord we just release that anointing upon them right now.

And the Lord says I have already answered your prayer for that personal situation. It is already being affected. I have angels on assignment, next week you will start hearing about what's taken place. And it is already beginning to work out. So trust me, believe me, and start praising me. Let your requests be made known now with thanksgiving, thanksgiving, thanksgiving, thanksgiving. Thank you Lord it is done. Thank you Lord you're doing it. Thank you Lord it is coming to pass.

For the Lord says now my son HEALING is going to start FLOWING through YOUR HANDS. I have given you that Apostolic gift of healing. And there are gifts of HEALING within you. And the healing Balm of Gilead is within you. So Lord I release not only the Prophetic in Sharon and the Revelation Word of Knowledge but I release healing and miracles in your servant and in your man of God, here Lord and your son. And I charge right now healing and revelation, let the gifts come forth in mighty power and in Jesus Name we thank you for it. AMEN and AMEN.

Chapter 9
My Testimony of Restoration

"For I know the plans I have for you," declares the Lord, "plans to prosper you and not to harm you, plans to give you hope and a future" (Jer. 29:11 NIV).

I was born July 18, 1953 in the state of West Virginia. My parents moved to Ohio when I was two years old. I was raised on a dairy farm in Northeastern Ohio. So yes, I can milk a cow. My parents both had full time jobs besides the dairy farm. So I was left alone a lot. I had an older sister and brother. My sister is twenty-five years older than me and my brother was twenty-three years older than me. They were both married with families when I was born. My older brother lived in Texas. My sister lived just up the road with her husband and children. So it was just me and my brother Delmas, who was five years older than me. Even at a young age he was always busy doing chores on the farm. So he was not always around. Therefore each of us had to take care of ourselves.

From the age of four to about eight I was sexually abused. My parents and brother never knew. My father worked for the railroad and he would leave on Sunday evening to go stay in a town about an hour away, so that he could leave in the early hours on Monday to go to wherever city he was needed. His job was to lay track for the railroad cars. Whenever there was a train wreck, a lot of times the track was tore up and destroyed. His job was very physical, laying those big railroad ties. For years, he only came home on Friday evening for the weekend. My mother worked very early in the morning until five o'clock. So my brother and I were pretty much on our own with no adult supervision. When I look at my grand children I could never imagine leaving them by themselves. But my parents did. I guess because of the way they were raised in West Virginia; it's what people did then. They didn't have a problem with it. They felt they had to do what they had to do, which was to provide a living for us. When my mom would leave for work in the morning, she would always tell me to be a good girl and watch TV, and she'd see me tonight. So, that is how the abuse could happen, because there were no adults around to protect me.

One of the questions that I used to ask myself when I got older is why didn't I tell my parents. One of the reasons was that I loved my parents so much that I didn't want to hurt them or be a bother to them. But the main reason was because I thought they wouldn't love me anymore. When you are sexually abused, it is not so much fear that keeps you from telling, it is shame. The spirit of shame told me it was my fault. I had such a spirit of shame from being sexually abused that I felt not even the Lord could love me. I remember as a little girl going to church, and wanting to be good so I could go to heaven. We attended a Quaker church. I thought there was no way God could ever love me, because I felt dirty. Though now I know it is not my fault and that I was the victim. There was a part of me that felt I was to blame. It wasn't until I got delivered from shame and fear that I realized I was just a little girl and could not have stopped it. I have had the privilege of teaching on abuse and bringing freedom to many people from the spirit of shame at conferences. What a turnaround that is, once I was a victim and had no voice, and now I am able to minister with compassion to deliver men and women from this torment.

It did not stop with the sexual abuse. Because I was not delivered and set free I had not only a spirit of shame, but also a spirit of victimization and abuse. When I married my late husband he was very worldly. As a child I spent hours and hours being babysat by the television. As I watched the weekly shows of big cities such as New York, there was a desire in me. I wanted to live in a city and have that kind of life, I saw these characters on TV, living. Not realizing that it wasn't real.

So when I met my late husband, he introduced me to that kind of life. He took me to the fancy restaurants, bought me presents and flowers. It was nothing like the simple life that I had lived on the farm. But it was similar to what I was used to watching on the television. The characters going out to dinner and having drinks, the man giving the woman presents, it seemed so enticing. I had never seen this in the natural. My parents had never gone out to dinner, and my father never brought my mom flowers. So now here I was living the life I thought I wanted. But my late husband was not a Christian. I found out early into the marriage he was very jealous. He would become so angry at me if anyone talked to me or visited me. We would have so many fights. I thought if I got pregnant it would help our marriage. Plus I wanted to have children.

I wanted to have my children when I was young so I could enjoy them. Unlike my parents when they had me.

My mom was forty-three and my father was almost fifty. So, I became pregnant a few months after our wedding and I was three months into the pregnancy when he hit me for the first time. I was totally shocked. Although we had lots of fights, up until that point, it was only verbal. I spent the next seventeen years being abused, not only physically but verbally and emotionally. The reason I never left or divorced him was that he vowed to kill me and the boys if I did. I believed him. He was that violent and full of rage.

It wasn't until I was in the deliverance ministry that I got a revelation of how strongholds work. Because I was abused sexually as a child, it set me up with not only shame, but also in my mind the thought that it was my fault. When my late husband hit me for the first time, what do you think he said to me? He said it was my fault. Had I not done so and so then he wouldn't have become angry and lost his temper. What that did was reinforce what the enemy had told me about the sexual abuse. That it was my fault and I somehow deserved it. The enemy set me up with a stronghold. When my late husband said those words of "it's your fault," then I thought I deserved it because I asked for it by not doing the right thing. Another thing the enemy would tell me was that it was because I was in rebellion when I married my late husband. I was not serving God at that time so it was rebellion. So that anything that happened to me was punishment for my sin. So there it was. I was being punished, and I deserved it. We know that is not how our Lord is. He would not want us to be abused, no matter what we did wrong. As a child though in the Quaker church, I only saw God as someone you didn't cross or get angry, because if you disobeyed Him there would be a price to pay.

In 1990 my late husband got saved. He was thirty-eight years old. Three weeks later he died of a fatal heart attack. Five years earlier I had rededicated my life to the Lord and had gotten spirit filled. I was attending a faith church at the time of my husband's death. Then two years earlier I had met a couple who were Christian International Ministers, Pastors Floyd and Sally Smith. What I didn't know is that God had them praying for me and my family. I know that I am alive today because of their faithfulness to pray for me. I am sure that the enemy had a plan, and he would have used my late husband to kill me, however, God had a purpose for my life. I started the chapter with the Scripture in Jeremiah 29:11, this is one of my favorite Scriptures, along with John 10:10, *"That the Lord had a purpose and a plan for me, it was for good and not evil, that I would have an abundant life."* What the enemy meant for harm, God turned it around and used it for His glory.

Eight months after my husband died, I moved to Santa Rosa Beach, Florida. I moved here to attend Christian International, and to be trained in the ministry. Even though I thought it was my idea to move here it was really the Lord's plan for me. He moved me here to not only train me and equip me but to heal me. Then several years later, he brought me my wonderful husband, Bob. When God restores, it is not just one area of our lives, it's in all areas. I not only got a godly husband, but my sons got a godly father. My parents were deceased, so when I married Bob I got parents again too. Helen and Adrian were Christians. They actually met in church in the youth group. Bob was raised in church. My mother-in-law told me he was only a few days old when she took him to church. When Bob and I married his parents moved to Florida to be close to us because he is an only child. We built a new house in 1998 and added on a place for them to live. Bob and his late wife had no children, and now he had three sons. Our son Daniel and his wife Casey have two children, Ashton and Clara. So Bob is not only a father but a grandfather also. This is what I meant when I said God restores not only in one area of our lives, but in all areas.

This is why I have such a passion for deliverance. I spent too many years being beat up in the natural and by the devil. Even as a born-again believer. I should have been walking in victory. When I tried to tell my old pastors and elders of what I was going through they would tell me that I just needed to have more faith. It wasn't about having more faith. It was about getting delivered, but they didn't believe in deliverance. So that set me up for a works mentality, if I fasted enough and prayed enough things would change. Things never did change. So then I felt frustrated that God was not answering my prayers. And it reinforced how I felt about myself, that it was what I deserved. It wasn't until I went through deliverance here in Florida with my Pastor Jane Hamon that I realized the truth. Truly, the truth does set you free, and I am free. While going through deliverance, Pastor Jane said to me when I listed pages of friends and relatives that had died in my life that she had never met anyone who had experienced that much death. Everything in our lives should line up with the Word of God. What most of us do is try to make the Word of God fit our experiences that we have gone through or are going through. So if things don't line up with God's Word we need to find out why and deal with it.

I want to see everyone walking in all that was purchased on the cross for them. I will be eternally grateful to the Lord for what he has done in my life. There is nothing like freedom. And deliverance is simple!

Chapter 10
The Prayers

Please feel free to use the following prayers as you minister unforgiveness and generational curses. I also have included a prayer to break off soul ties.

Some people are not aware of the term "soul ties." When the Lord created marriage, it was so that we would be one with our mate. Matthew 19:4-6 says, *"And He answered and said to them, "Have you not read that He who made them at the beginning 'made them male and female,' [5]and said, 'For this reason a man shall leave his father and mother and be joined to his wife, and the two shall become one flesh'? [6]So then, they are no longer two but one flesh. Therefore what God has joined together, let not man separate."*

Do you not know that your bodies are members of Christ? Shall I then take the members of Christ and make them members of a harlot? Certainly not! [16]Or do you not know that he who is joined to a harlot is one body with her? For "the two," He says, "shall become one flesh." [17]But he who is joined to the Lord is one spirit with Him (1 Cor. 6:15-17).

The Lord created sex to be contained within the institution of marriage so that we can become one, but many have had sexual relationships outside of marriage. This means that they have become one with more people than their spouse. Sometimes with numerous people. But we can break off that connection that they had made with others by praying this prayer.

Breaking Soul Ties Prayer
"Lord, in the name of JESUS, I submit my spirit, soul, and body to you. I confess, as sin all my sexual relationships outside of marriage. I confess all of my ungodly spirit, soul, and body ties as sin. I forgive those with whom I have committed these sins and for whatever part they played and I release them. I repent of my involvement in all ungodly soul ties and I ask You to forgive me Lord. Father I break my ungodly soul tie with (name of those involved) and I release myself from them and them from me. I sever that linking supernaturally and ask You Lord to remove from me all the influence of them and drawback to myself every part that was wrongfully tied in bondage to another person. I loose myself now and ask You to come Holy Spirit and heal my mind so that I am set free to give my soul totally to God and to my mate. Father I receive Your forgiveness of all past sexual sins, and I forgive myself for these sins. I thank You for remembering them no more and for cleansing me from all unrighteousness. AMEN."

This is just one more area that we take back from the enemy and it brings a release of freedom. The same happens with the generational curses prayer and unforgiveness.

Forgiving Others Prayer

The deliverance minister needs to explain about forgiveness to the person being delivered. Read them the Scripture in Mark 11:26. God says if we don't forgive He won't forgive us.

"And his master was angry, and delivered him to the torturers until he should pay all that was due to him. [35] *'So My heavenly Father also will do to you if each of you, from his heart, does not forgive his brother his trespasses'"* (Matthew 18:34-35).

This Scripture in Matthew plainly states that God not only will not forgive us but he will turn this over to the tormentors or torturers. Does that sound like demons to you? God is serious about this. We tell them forgiveness is not an emotion but a decision. We ask them if they are able to forgive before we take them through deliverance. If not, they need to cancel their appointment until such time they can do this because it will open them up for more oppression if they do not forgive. There has been an exception to this rule as the Holy Spirit has occasionally told us that we need to cast out the spirit of unforgiveness so that they are able to forgive. But as I said, this only happens occasionally.

Have them repeat this prayer:
> "Lord, I lift up (name of person they need to forgive) to You. Lord, You said if I don't forgive them, You won't forgive me. So I choose to forgive (name of person they need to forgive) now. I release them Lord to You. I ask You to come Holy Spirit and heal my emotions and memory of all that happened, and of the incident. God, forgive me for any way I have partnered in an ungodly way with unforgiveness, bitterness, anger, or resentment toward them."

Now the deliverance minister prays for a healing of the memory concerning what happened so that when they remember it, it will no longer have any sting. Also they pray for a healing of the emotions whether it be anger, hate, or resentment, etc.

Generational Curses Prayer

Generational curses are the sins that our ancestors have committed, and then Satan passes that same sin onto us. If we do not break it, it will then be passed on to our descendants. Exodus 20:5 says, *"For I the Lord thy God am a jealous God, visiting the iniquity of the fathers upon the children unto the 3rd and 4th generation of them that hate me."* So we need to break any generational curses we see in the family line.

Have them repeat this prayer.
> "Father God, Creator of heaven and earth, I come before You now and I confess all the sins of my ancestors. Lord I forgive them for this sin and I ask You to forgive them also. Lord I also ask You to forgive me for anyway I have participated in their sin. Jesus I thank You that when you died on the cross, You became a curse for me. So now I apply that blood to wash away all generational curses. Thank You Jesus. AMEN."

Deliverance minister now prays this over the person receiving ministry.
> "I thank You Lord for freedom from (list all generational curses here that the Holy Spirit is showing you) and we shut the door to all their effects on this Godly vessel. I cancel all dedications or ungodly covenants their ancestors may have made. I thank You Lord that they are in a new family of God

where there are no generational sins and curses only generational blessing. AMEN."

We say deliverance is easy but walking out the freedom is the hard part. People can stay free if they follow the directions given to us by the Lord in His Word. Which is, forsaking not the assembling together, and keeping the Ten Commandments. Also, they need to have a strong prayer life and worship the Lord daily. This is the penicillin that will keep the infection away. Or as we say it is the Gos-pill.

I hope that this book and prayers in it will be an inspiration, and a tool for you to set the captives free and bring total liberty to those once held in bondage; to see that deliverance can be and is simple. And that you will now have a revelation of true deliverance.

You can contact Sharon and her husband Bob at:
Sharon Parkes
email: Isaiah624@aol.com
web site: www.Isaiah624.org

Made in the USA
Columbia, SC
26 September 2022